Anne Rice and Sexual Politics

The Early Novels

by JAMES R. KELLER

with Conclusion by
JAMES R. KELLER *and* GWENDOLYN MORGAN

McFarland & Company, Inc., Publishers
Jefferson, North Carolina, and London

ISBN 0-7864-0846-4 (softcover : 50# alkaline paper) ∞

Library of Congress cataloguing data are available

British Library cataloguing data are available

Manufactured in the United States of America

*McFarland & Company, Inc., Publishers
 Box 611, Jefferson, North Carolina 28640
  www.mcfarlandpub.com*

CONTENTS

INTRODUCTION:
FASHIONING THE AUTHOR

The vampire Louis in Anne Rice's first novel, *Interview with the Vampire*, experiences some adjustment issues in his transition from living to undead. His lingering humanity will not permit him to kill for his own sustenance. He is encumbered in his overpowering desire for human blood by a lingering sense of moral duty and by his addiction to humanity's ethical structures, even after he realizes that those constructs have no remaining application to his life. He struggles to maintain his humanity through his ostensible commitment to social contracts—restraint of passion and respect for life. Representative of the Freudian split consciousness, he is defined by the struggle between his desire to indulge his libidinal impulses and his compulsion to obey social strictures. Indeed, the novel itself could be characterized as a narrative of liberation in which Louis comes to a complete acceptance of his vampire nature or perhaps his animal/libidinal nature.

Anne Rice has been very insistent in her personal identification with Louis. She even suggested that the vampire be cast as a female in an early movie script in order to resolve the gender controversies that held up production of the film for almost twenty years. Louis' moral reticence in the face of a powerful desire is his defining characteristic, and we can see this same quality in Rice's public persona. Through both her novels and her interviews, Rice persistently pays homage to a polymorphous sexuality as well as a variety of marginalized subject positions, yet she also undermines the authenticity of these portrayals with the conventionality of her life and her narrative conclusions, consigning these subject positions to the realm of fiction and artifice.

Because the subject matter of her novels is frequently unconventional and many of her characters are representative of the socially marginal, one might expect that the author shares a peculiar propensity for nonconformity. This, however, does not seem to be the case. While there is little or no moral condemnation of her characters, there is a refusal, both in her fiction and in the rhetoric of her public persona, to embrace a revolutionary posture toward social marginality. Upon a superficial consideration, Rice seems to be quite radical in her views toward sex and in her willingness to represent the sexual outsiders in her fiction. However, even here there is a narrative bias toward normative conclusions, such as marriage. Frequently in her work, erotic experimentation is valued exclusively for its impact upon monogamous relations. Even her most dedicated proponents of free love eventually discover that only marriage is truly satisfactory. The protagonists of *Exit to Eden* abandon their commitment to multiple partners and same-sex relations for traditional matrimony. At the conclusion of *The Erotic Adventures of Sleeping Beauty*, Beauty and Laurent exploit their countless sexual experiences, as well as the self-discipline that is an integral part of their S & M training, to the benefit of their conventional monogamous match. In the midst of their multifarious erotic adventures, the characters of Rice's *Beauty* series long for a meaningful relationship with a single individual. Even Rice's vampires desire a partner with whom they might endure eternity, and although these relations exist within a virtual orgy of erotic experiences, the vampires are nevertheless portrayed as partners who share many of the characteristics of conventional marriage.

In her public persona, Rice pays homage to alternative sexual identities. Yet her own relations and sexual propensities are ostensibly quite conventional. She praises sexual experimentation, but she has remained dedicated to the same partner her entire adult life and seems to be exceptionally family oriented. Rice writes extensively about the practices of S & M and even offers a defense of these experiences based upon their potentially therapeutic value, yet the author admits to her biographer that she balked at the offer to meet directly with S & M practitioners. Indeed, her reason for refusing the offer closely resembles disdain: "I just couldn't do it ... I didn't want to know them that well," she says, further distancing herself from S & M activities by suggesting that her brief encounters with "those people" actually resulted in the discontinuation of the *Beauty* series after the third book (Ramsland *Prism* 242–43). Clearly, Rice was willing to defend the practices of S & M in the abstract and to exploit the subject for its market value, but when confronted with the actuality of the practice, she experiences something akin to moral revulsion. Her husband defends her against the accusation that she is a dominatrix: "She's no more sadomasochistic than she's a vampire" (Ramsland, *Prism* 243). This vindication constitutes a defense of the conventionality of the author's sex life, as though those marginal erotic practices that she so lovingly describes in her work are something to be shunned and repudiated.

Frequently, her representations of homosexuality involve a similar propensity for the conventional. In her erotic literature, same-sex eroticism is merely experimental, a propensity that may be morally neutral but which is something to be transcended. Both Lisa and Eliot, the protagonists of *Exit to Eden*, abandon their same-sex desires for a conventional monogamous bond with a member of the opposite sex. The protagonists of the *Beauty* series also forsake their homosexual practices for the normative heterosexual marriage. Other characters who engage in homosexual encounters are essentially bisexual. Christophe from *The Feast of All Saints* abandons his homosexual lover Michael to return to New Orleans, and once home, he immediately seeks sexual gratification from Dolly Rose, a loose woman of color. Rice's vampires form same-sex bonds, but they can never be fully identified as homosexual. Although there is a noticeable dearth of female characters in the *Vampire Chronicles*, there is nevertheless an implication that a member of either gender would constitute a sufficient partner with whom to endure eternity. Although one might argue that the mere suggestion that a same-sex bond is an acceptable choice constitutes a progressive position on gender issues, representations of those who have exclusively homosexual attractions are conspicuously absent from her early texts.

Rice's argument that the immersion in the flesh leads to spiritual transcendence also has a conservative subtext. Although she asserts that the indulgence of the flesh through sex and bondage constitutes a pathway to spiritual awakening, she nevertheless advocates a novel process with a conventional objective. The process merely exploits the body for the attainment of something that transcends body: the spiritual or the intellectual. This does not constitute a dramatic break from the Western philosophical tradition that one must forsake the flesh to experience enlightenment. It argues instead that the path to that forsaking is through the flesh itself and through the surrender of the body and the volition to the will of another. Thus, rather than truly embracing the flesh and subsequently the erotic, Rice's philosophical position merely represents yet another means of denying the flesh in favor of that which transcends it, this time paradoxically through meaningless carnal indulgence. Is this total satiation of the flesh not another means of repudiating the flesh, of representing it as negligible, as a means to a more meaningful indulgence?

At every level, Rice can be observed to negotiate between a radical and a conventional point of view regarding sex and social taboo. In Michael Riley's *Conversations with Anne Rice*, Rice asserts that she finds the pictures of naked children in *Vogue* "very erotic." She then goes on to describe the "sensuous enjoyment" that she experiences when showering her children with kisses and hugs, initially a rather bold admission from a mother and a mainstream writer. However, in her subsequent explanation, she very rapidly distances herself from any impropriety, so much so that she completely eviscerates the concept of the erotic, implying that she means nothing more unconventional than maternal affection, an interest in watching her son grow "big and strong" (63–65). The backpedaling is very clear in the exchange. The author wants credit for the shocking suggestion, but she does not want to face the social stigma that would attend such an admission. It is easy to understand that she would not want to associate herself with a practice as ignominious as pedophilia, particularly when it carries the additional stigma of incest. However, the author wants to raise eyebrows and to perpetuate an outrageous public persona, and yet at the same time, she does not want to be taken seriously. In her fiction and in her initial assertions about children, she appears to be endorsing pedophilic desire. Yet she very plainly backs away from the idea as well, thus complying with conventional concepts of propriety. In her fiction, the instances of intergenerational eroticism are legion (e.g., Belinda, Beauty, Mona, Armand, etcetera). The author even offers a defense of such sexual desire in her biography *Prism of the Night*, where she suggests that some children are mature enough to negotiate a sexual relationship with an adult and that sometimes the child is even the aggressor (52). If Rice were to leave these ideas in the world of her fiction, there would be no issue. However, she clearly considers the idea a philosophical position about sexual repression in our society, and she even flirts with the concept in the public characterizations that she makes of her family. Yet as with other issues, the ideas are not ones that she is entirely capable of owning. She recoils from any public conviction on the subject. It becomes clear that she does not really accept the very ideas that she wants the public to believe that she is very comfortable with. Thus she is fashioning a fallacious public posture as the sexual outlaw. The argument that she is not obliged to be what she writes does not particularly apply because authors of erotica have often been defined by the stigma associated with their subject. Also, the effort to define her public image as an eccentric and a sexual dissident erases the dividing line between her fiction and her reality.

A similar duality in her public persona could be observed in a recent interview. When the author appeared on Brian Lamb's television program

Booknotes to promote her work *Servant of the Bones*, she wore the garments that one might expect her characters to wear, a dark velvet dress replete with lace fringe and other accessories reminiscent of eighteenth-century fashion. It was clear that her intention had been to dress in character, to reinforce public perceptions that she is more than a little eccentric, that she is subversive of middle-class values, particularly sexual prohibitions, and that she may even be a little dangerous. Yet despite her nonconformist persona, she insisted on talking to the interviewer about tax reform, a subject that one would expect from an accountant, not from the author of horror and erotic fiction. The interviewer's consternation was obvious even to Rice, yet he was unable to bring her back to the subject of her fiction. Plainly, the author only flirts with the revolutionary; her inclination is consistently toward the mundane.

Despite her long residence in San Francisco, even during the period of the psychedelic cultural awakening, Rice did not adopt a slavish adherence to radical leftist politics. She recognizes that the political spectrum is not linear but circular, with the extremity of the Left touching the extremity of the Right. Hippies and Berkeley intellectuals, she complains, were frequently indistinguishable from fascists in their sentiments toward the political opposition. She adds incredulously that the California intellectual's notion of liberalism is to torture and kill a conservative, and she refers to Berkeleyites as "merciless," "dangerous," and "vicious." She complains of a professor who talked of abducting and killing the wife of a prominent conservative politician to protest the Vietnam War. She also describes with disdain the hypocrisy of Californian Marxists, many of whom have never had to work, living off of trust funds while offering impassioned speeches on the plight of the migrant farmhands. The communist system itself does not escape her criticism. She boldly labels it "ruthless" and "guilty of mass murder" (Riley 149–55).

Rice's resentment toward leftist politics does not signify conservative leanings. She fashions herself as a liberal, adopting leftist positions on many social issues. A self-styled humanitarian, Rice suggests that to be an intellectual and to be liberal is to adopt a respect and appreciation for diverse, and even radically opposing, points of view. However, this does not necessarily mean that she is a traditional moderate, particularly on sexual issues, but that she has respect for the free exchange of ideas. She is most angry with liberals when they ally themselves, or adopt the practices commonly associated, with right-wing politics. Feminism, a movement that one would expect a successful woman such as Anne Rice to embrace wholeheartedly, has been a frequent target of her admonitions. In her opinion, the sexual politics of feminists such as Catherine

MacKinnon and Andrea Dworkin are allied with right-wing patriarchal values. MacKinnon's and Dworkin's views on the exploitation of women through pornography reveal a subtle hatred of women's sexuality. These writers suggest that the women depicted in pornographic film are whores because they appear to enjoy anonymous sex or are exploited. No liberated woman would ever willingly participate in a pornographic production. Rice denounces this point of view for the same reason that she rejects sexism: because it limits women's choices, telling them "what they should feel" and condemning those who do not conform to prescribed philosophy (Ramsland *Prism* 218).

Rice's choice of subject matter reveals a negotiation between high and low culture, between the elite and the popular, between literature and commercial fiction. While many consider her career a surrender to the latter item in each of the above categories, such generalizations oversimplify the contents of her work, which is better characterized as a constant oscillation between high and low or as a recurring penetration of the boundaries between the oppositions. Rice's books are novels of ideas. They demonstrate an impressive understanding of art, literature, philosophy, psychology, and history. However, they are also generally an effort to appeal to the readers of the commercial marketplace. Rice was surprised and disappointed when she did not receive recognition as a serious writer after the publication and success of her first novel, *Interview with the Vampire*. The subjects of her next two novels reveal that literary respectability was not only her objective, but also her due. She was astonished that her first novel could be dismissed by critics and reviewers simply because she chose to exploit the genre of horror fiction, and her point is well taken. While the adoption of the vampire story is often correctly conceived as a signal of the author's desire to appeal to a mass audience, such considerations do not necessarily subvert the effort to make thoughtful observations about art, philosophy, and life. Within the context of a vampire story, *Interview* addresses a multiplicity of literary thematics, including the anxieties of immortality, the search for identity, the problems of domestic abuse, and the relationships between art, reality, mythology, and folklore. Moreover, these ideas are set against a rich eighteenth-century backdrop that reveals an appreciation for historical detail and an understanding of the spirit of the age.

Her subsequent novels are equally persistent in their appropriation of the high and the low. Rice's publisher tried to explain the initial commercial failure of her second novel *The Feast of All Saints* by theorizing that "it fell between the literary and the popular, and people just did not know what to do with it" (Ramsland *Prism* 192). *The Vampire Lestat* and

Queen of the Damned contain lengthy recreations of ancient fertility cults and mythologies. Yet the impressive anthropological detail of the historical sections is countered by the vulgar, even comic framing device of Lestat as a rock star, flaunting his vampirism to the outrage of his supernatural colleagues.

This conflict between conformity and revolution and between high and low culture can be observed throughout Rice's early fiction. The term "early" is used rather loosely in this study, referring to texts written between 1976, the publication of *Interview*, and 1993, the publication of *Lasher*. This study acknowledges that the quality of any author's work varies, but that with Rice the variation is perhaps more pronounced. Some of her novels possess intellectual and aesthetic qualities that achieve literary status, while others seem to be little more than escapist fiction. Moreover, the author seems to have lost her ability to distinguish between the high and the low as it is represented in her individual works. She will make disparaging remarks about the shortcomings of her most worthy novels (*The Feast of All Saints* and *Cry to Heaven*), while praising books that are virtually bankrupt of merit. She complains that the novel *Cry to Heaven*, a compelling historical work about the castrated singers in the Italian opera, took too long to get to the central action of the conservatory. Yet at the same time, she maintains that the novel *The Mummy*, a work that makes no pretense to the literary, was worthy of a sequel (Ramsland *Prism* 323). Plainly, the commercial and the meritorious have become coterminous in the author's mind, a progression that has become increasingly apparent as her career degenerates into a series of rapidly assembled codicils to her early successes. Having already related the heart of the vampire Armand's history in one of her early novels, she nevertheless deems the subject worthy of additional treatment, creating a book that narrates around the edges of the previously told tale. In her recent work *Pandora*, she creates an entire book around a story that does not have sufficient subject matter to warrant a digression in one of her previous novels. Yet even in her most commercial efforts, she frequently generates vividly conceived images of historical epochs or weaves into her narrative thoughtful philosophical meditations.

Each chapter of this study will observe the author's negotiation between the urge to conform to and the compulsion to subvert traditional bourgeois values about sexuality and gender. For example, the gay and lesbian community has been very quick to identify with Rice's vampires, reading the series as a lengthy allegory of sexual dissidence and social stigma. Chapter 1, "Interrogating the Vampire: Heterotextuality and Queer Reading," exposes the ways in which such a reading perpetuates destructive, indefensible stereotypes about the gay community. All of the common insults are represented: promiscuity, predacious sexuality, pedophilia, melancholia, self-destructiveness, et cetera. Moreover, in a political environment laden with homophobic rhetoric that characterizes gays and lesbians as incompatible with family life, the representation of the vampire family as a collection of monsters who invert all of the traditional familial relations is particularly repugnant and even dangerous. The chapter demonstrates that such readings are noxious to the struggle for human rights.

Chapter 2, "Engendering Whiteness: The Politics of Race, Gender, and Class in *The Feast of All Saints*," addresses the social construction of racial ideology. The novel focuses on a group of free people of color living in New Orleans before the Civil War. Borrowing from psychoanalytic and feminist traditions, this chapter observes the relationship between patriarchy and racial and gender discrimination. I argue that *The Feast of All Saints* dismantles the ideology of racial difference in American culture, erasing ethnic boundaries and exposing the vacuum at the center of patriarchal power. Like the Lacanian phallus, whiteness exists only as an ideal that is defined entirely by its opposition to other ethnic categories. It is the point at which the endless significations of racial difference begin. White is not a biological classification. It is an artificial category that social and economic factors have created, and one into which no character actually fits within the novel. Many of the social codes that are associated with whiteness are more prominent among the people of color than among the Caucasians. Moreover, the Caucasians invariably fall short of that ideal of power, privilege, and affluence that defines whiteness. The characters struggle to define themselves racially by embarking on a breeding program in which their progeny will be indistinguishable from the white population, but the irony of their efforts is that whiteness is only a mirage.

Chapter 3, "The Purloined Penis: Castration Anxiety in *Cry to Heaven*," is an application of the theories of Jacques Lacan as articulated in his "Seminar on *The Purloined Letter*" where he suggests that meaning and identity are determined by the subject's position within the signifying chain. In *Cry to Heaven*, four members of the same family compose four separate oedipal triangles. As the characters move from one position in the family romance to another, their perceptions of themselves as subjects alter as well. Tonio's castration constitutes a displacement not only within the social, political, and economic sphere, but also within the system of signification. For Tonio, the movement through all of the positions of the family romance constitutes a realization of his latent androgyny. However, Rice's incipient sexual conservatism undermines much of the revolutionary potential of such a discovery.

Few subjects inspire as much intransigence and hysteria as the sexual initiation of children. Yet Rice frequently embraces the topic and offers some quite heretical views. Chapter 4, "Violation and Sex Education: Beauty's Erotic Odyssey," examines the sexual politics of this incendiary subject as it is addressed in Rice's erotic and sadomasochistic rewriting of the Sleeping Beauty fairy tale. The author seeks to demonstrate that childhood is fraught with sexuality and that parents ignore the obvious saturation of childhood with carnal desire to maintain the fiction that children are pure, empty of sexual cravings. Rice even takes the radical step of suggesting that the sexual initiation of children may be beneficial, instructing them in discipline and self-control. However, as with all of her boldest affirmations, she shies away from any unrepentantly revolutionary stands about sex. She examines the initiation of children in the knowledge of the flesh as an introduction to a normative bourgeois lifestyle that is replete with traditional marriage and gender inequity.

Chapter 5, *Exit to Eden*: The Body, the Spectacle, and the Transgressive Space," is a Bakhtinian analysis of sexual transgression and the carnivalesque. It examines the containment of subversive energies within the same apparatus that threatens to undermine civil authority, and it focuses on attributes of the carnival such as the flouting of authority, the spectacle of the grotesque body, and the celebration of fertility. The chapter deconstructs the oppositions generated by sadomasochistic practice. The values of pleasure/pain and liberty/constraint are inverted, and the border between antithetical concepts dissolves. In *Exit to Eden*, Rice is carnivalizing the carnival, reversing the priorities of the historical celebration by employing the subversive traditions to their own destruction. Such a praxis is conservative if it undercuts an exercise that is reverent and seditious. It begins with what seems to be a radical, revolutionary agenda for sexual liberation and concludes with a conventional marital union.

Chapter 6, "Prurient Painters and Pedophiles: Negotiating Consent in *Belinda*," reveals Rice's effort to navigate between two ill-defined forms of intergenerational sex: pedophilia and child molestation. Rice's confidence that an adolescent has the ability to consent to sexual relations with an adult is the crux upon which she distinguishes between nurturing and destructive intergenerational bonds. The example of the precocious and resourceful Belinda is intended to invalidate the assumption that all pedophilic relations are exploitative of, and harmful toward, the child. While the author makes an effort to diminish the transgressive potential of the subject by excluding explicit descriptions of sex and by constructing a relationship that will end in a permanent monogamous bond between the participants, she nevertheless confronts a virtually insurmountable cultural bias against her thesis, one that promises to silence and invalidate any such narratives. At another level, the novel is a thinly veiled allegory of the risks that Rice took in publishing her erotica, particularly the erotica that depicts relations between adults and children. Thus, the novel becomes a defense of the writer's aesthetic judgment in the selection of subject matter, even that material that may be socially taboo.

Chapter 7, "Rape Fantasies: Constructing a Masculine Prototype Among the Mayfair Witches" is an application of the theories of contemporary men's studies. Traditionally, our culture has defined manhood very narrowly, allowing only a quite limited group of characteristics to be coded as truly masculine. Inspired by feminism, men's studies seeks to identify and legitimize a plurality of masculine types. In *The Lives of the Mayfair Witches*, Rice attempts to deconstruct the reductive notions of masculinity that have characterized traditional gender coding. Rice's two principal male characters are an effort to broaden the scope of acceptable masculine practice. Michael is represented as genteel brute; he has an uncommon sensitivity and a coarser side that makes him sexually exciting. In appearance, Lasher is more androgynous than Michael is, and yet Lasher retains the sexual aggressiveness and self-centeredness that is historically associated with hegemonic masculinity. Rice's rehabilitation of masculinity, however, does not disempower or emasculate the male characters as much as it advocates the strengthening of the female characters. Rowan is representative of the woman who can compete with men at every level: intellectually, emotionally, and physically.

It is clear in her choice of subjects that the author desires to challenge the boundaries of sexual tolerance. Yet she is consistently unwilling to step boldly over the line, and it is just this trepidation that the current study seeks to observe. The publication of some of the novels was in and of itself an act of subversion. The fact that the author occasionally chose a pseudonym reveals her initial reticence, her unwillingness to defy convention openly. She can write shamelessly of Prince Alexi and the stone phallus, but only after the portrayal gains some level of public acceptance is she willing to reveal her authorship. Like Louis, she hides her perversity and pays homage to convention and society's moral constructs.

Chapter 1

INTERROGATING THE VAMPIRE: HETEROTEXTUALITY AND QUEER READING

In an article entitled "On Becoming a Lesbian Reader," Alison Hennegan suggests that the process of queer reading involves a search for the occulted expression of lesbian and gay sensibilities, even when those expressions must be manufactured through the most rigorous textual exegesis. Feminist critics have recognized that the interpretation of women's issues in literature has often involved the careful analysis of their exclusion from the text. Feminists have thus focused on the gaps where women might have been represented or have even been forced to posit male characters as representations of the female identity. Gay and lesbian readers have found themselves in very much the same predicament. Although the Western canon has been far more open in the expression of deep sentiment between same-sex partners than has the culture itself, the representations of forbidden desire have often been veiled and obscured. The publication of some of the nineteenth century's best-known texts about same-sex relations have been accompanied by the authors' explicit denials of homoerotic content. I speak of Tennyson's *In Memoriam* and Whitman's *Calamus Poems*. Both authors, in compliance with contemporary prohibitions against homosexual content in art, repudiate the queer reading of their work. However, such readings persist, consigning the author's denials to obligatory observance of the culturally imposed silence upon the issue.

Arguing against the idea that Western culture has been sexually repressed, Michel Foucault observes that the history of sexuality since the enlightenment has involved the proliferation of veiled discourses about sex (Foucault *History of Sexuality Vol. I*). Various theoretical schools have adopted this position in their critical practice, observing the covert manifestations of repressed sexuality. Queer theory, following Foucault's lead, has sought to unmask allegories of gender and sexuality within both canonical and popular texts. Minority literary studies have tended to concentrate on noncanonical texts because the sociopolitical preoccupations of the traditional canon have tended to prioritize white, male, heterosexist subjectivity. The queer critiques that have focused on traditional texts have frequently been confined to an examination of the hetero/phallocentrality of the work. Such studies adopt exegetical practices that are similar to feminist theory by addressing the meaningful absence of relevant gender issues. Queer literary studies have examined the homoerotic implications of same-sex relations that involve little or no sexual content. Examples include studies of the assumed homoerotic attraction of Claggert to Billy Budd and of Nick's obsessive interest in Gatsby in Fitzgerald's classic novel. Such studies have proven remarkably enlightening in the revelation of character and gender relations. However, in the effort to unmask the traces of same-sex passion, queer theorists have requisitioned and endorsed texts that prove obnoxious to gay and lesbian sexual politics, texts that tend to reinforce destructive stereotypes and that are hostile to the struggle for social equality.

For the past century, representations of the vampire have proven remarkably fecund in their ability to generate new allegorical significations. The vampire myth has remained adaptable to the constant proliferation of contemporaneous issues. Perhaps those studies that have identified the monster as a manifestation of unconscious fears and desires have managed to locate the source of the character's continuing appeal (Gelder 17). It is certainly true that critics have made the vampire jump through a myriad of interpretive hoops. The monster has become an emblem of class and race struggles, of xenophobia, of the Cold War, of the conflict between science and superstition, and of erotic relations. It is on the latter of these issues that this discussion will focus.

Gay and lesbian readers have been quick to identify with the representation of the vampire, suggesting its experiences parallel those of the sexual outsider. In his article "Children of the Night," Richard Dyer summarizes many of the recurring homoerotic motifs of vampire fiction. Chief among these are the necessity of secrecy, the persistence of a forbidden passion, and the fear of discovery (64). Ken Gelder's book *Reading the Vampire* also addresses the same-sex eroticism of vampire fiction. His treatment of the subject concentrates mostly on J. Sheridan Le Fanu's "Carmilla" (Gelder 58–64) and Anne Rice's *The Vampire Chronicles* (Gelder

108–23). Terri R. Liberman, in her article "Eroticism as the Moral Fulcrum in Rice's *Vampire Chronicles*," maintains that the violation of moral taboos, particularly erotic ones, is the most engaging feature of Rice's vampire novels. Liberman particularly identifies homosexuality as the principal violation of social norms (109). What is most remarkable about such studies is that they fail to recognize the homophobic implications of such portrayals. For decades, gays and lesbians have rigorously policed the media's depictions of alternative lifestyles through the watchdog group Gay and Lesbian Alliance Against Defamation (GLAAD). Yet the widespread identification with vampire fiction has remained unquestioned. Perhaps allegorical obscurity and the fantastic nature of the character makes the negative implications of the parallel less menacing.

The publication of Rice's *The Vampire Chronicles* has done much to reinforce the widely recognized parallel between the queer and the vampire. Ken Gelder categorizes Rice's readers into two groups: the gay audience and the mainstream audience (118). John Preston, a writer and friend of Rice's, delineates the appeal of the author's vampire fiction to the gay community:

> The passage about initiation ... and the concepts of being separate from society—perhaps even above it, but always estranged by it—fit most gay men's self-images. Many gay men find the descriptions about becoming a vampire to be parallel to coming out, especially involving the welcome seduction by a being who holds the secret to the future. Gay men also relate to the voluptuousness of the descriptions and the heavy sensuality [quoted in Ramsland *Prism* 266].

Numerous reviewers have recognized and even promoted this parallel with the gay lifestyle, identifying with the creatures' "guilt, alienation, and ... struggle with ... deviance" (Ramsland *Prism* 148). Jerry Douglas of the *Washington Post* observed that *The Vampire Chronicles* "constitute[s] one of the most extended metaphors in modern literature." In a refreshingly critical view of the parallel, Leo Braudy of the *New York Times Book Review* observes that "homosexuality ... is the hardly hidden mainspring of Rice's narrative, and her message seems to be: if you're homosexual, it's better to be unemotional about it" (quoted in Ramsland *Prism* 169). In her book *Our Vampires Ourselves*, Nina Auerbach devotes an entire chapter to the parallels between vampires and homosexuality; she is particularly interested in the representation of the AIDS pandemic in vampire fiction, including Rice's *The Vampire Chronicles* (Auerbach 163–92).

Hollywood evidently recognized the homoerotic content of *Interview with the Vampire* when it bought the rights in 1976. The delay in the creation of the film, which did not appear until 1994, resulted from Paramount Pictures' inability to market a story that involved an erotic triangle between two men and a child (Ramsland *Prism* 264). The effort to bring the novel to the screen included many script revisions that were intended to sanitize the story for the popular viewing audience. One script made Daniel (the interviewer) and Armand into young women and made the child, Claudia, into an eighteen-year-old woman. Rice complained that the story had been eviscerated. The author then suggested that the screenplay make Louis a woman because the gender transformation would be consistent with his passivity (Ramsland *Prism* 268–69). This alteration never materialized. It turns out that what the novel needed to be made more palatable was 20 years of social change and the subsequent increased tolerance toward gays and lesbians. It is probably no accident that Neil Jordan, who popularized transvestism, transsexualism, and same-sex desire with his film *The Crying Game*, was the one to bring *Interview with the Vampire* to the screen with all of the original gender roles intact.

This chapter will concentrate primarily on the first novel within the series, with brief excursions into the subsequent novels, exploiting them for illustrations and traces of unraveling narrative structures. The intention of the discussion is not to sound the presence of each and every manifestation of same-sex desire (although some of this will be necessary to accomplish the chapter's project), but to expose the destructive ramifications of the queer reading of the text. With this critical objective the discussion becomes somewhat paradoxical. As I attempt to demonstrate the destructive potential of a queer reading of the text, I will be making the most extensive delineation of the motif thus far.

It is certainly not my intention to accuse the author of conscious homophobia, but to suggest that she has internalized heterosexist paradigms and has unconsciously represented them in her novel. I also submit that the demands of the literary marketplace necessitate conventional heterocentric conclusions. Anne Rice has had a long association with the gay community, which includes keeping her residence for many years in the Castro district of San Francisco. In addition, she has broken the culturally imposed silence upon the issue of homosexuality in virtually every one of her novels, a move that is both bold and socially significant in popular fiction because it is obligatory silence that perpetuates repression and myth.

An interrogation of the queer reading of *Interview* must begin with the issue that delayed the production of the film for over 15 years: the vampire family. In the current American political climate, a domestic group that is plainly a demonic inversion of the traditional bourgeois family generates many highly negative implications. The conservative campaign for protecting "family values," a program that has vexed the gay and lesbian community for several decades, has coded the same-sex unit as anathema to all that is healthy and natural. In right-wing politics, the homosexual became the new evil icon after the collapse of the Soviet Union, allowing conservative demagogues to consolidate their power by manipulating the irrational fears of the populace. In such a hostile political atmosphere, the queer reading of *Interview* seems to play right into the hands of those most determined to inhibit the struggle for social equality. The homophobic interpretation of the same-sex unit has long assumed that queer relationships are merely a grotesque parody of the normative bourgeois couple, and the queer reading of Rice's vampire family reinforces that interpretation.

Ken Gelder identifies the domestic unit of Lestat, Louis, and Claudia as the "queer family" (Gelder 113), and it is certainly true that Rice has gone out of her way to make the vampire clan into a representation of the quintessential dysfunctional family, replete with domestic abuse and justifiable homicide. All of the conventions of the normative family unit have been inverted. Lestat stalks rather than courts Louis, and the "dark trick" that transforms Louis into a vampire resembles a rape more than it does a marriage and consummation. The homoerotic imagery associated with Louis' conversion has been a significant feature of the queer reading of the text. Lestat comes to Louis in his bed and hovers over him. Louis admits that the experience was "not unlike the pleasure of passion" (19), and he tells the young interviewer that to articulate his conversion would be as difficult as describing sex to someone who has never experienced it. Of course, in this parody of the traditional marriage, the couple never again share the erotic experience after their initial consummation. The marriage ceremony is supposed to initiate new life, but in the vampire story, the union signifies death and sterility.

According to Louis' account, Lestat has chosen him for all of the wrong reasons. Louis believes that his partner only desires his wealth, and his Pointe du Lac plantation (13). Indeed, their lives together do initially resemble the arranged, aristocratic marriages of the eighteenth century, one in which the bond has been created to consolidate family wealth. The young, discontented, neglected wife remains at home while the dissolute husband goes out marauding every night, squandering the collective fortune. Later in the novel, Louis indicates that Lestat only remains with him because the elder vampire is utterly incompetent in financial matters and requires Louis to handle the money. Of course, Louis' interpretation of Lestat's motivations runs counter to that offered by Lestat in the second novel, where he maintains that he chose Louis because the aristocrat reminded him of Nicholas, a young and sensitive musician whom Lestat once loved.

In her portrayal of the vampire family, Rice universalizes the male-female and aggressive-passive binarisms of heterosexual unions. Lestat possesses traditional male attributes, such as aggression, bluntness, insensitivity, and practicality. Louis is feminized, manifesting traits such as passivity, sensitivity, compunction, compassion, and resentment (Gelder 112). Furthermore, the marital roles of the two vampires reinforce the nineteenth-century distinction between the separate spheres of men and women. Socially and historically constituted gender constructions designated the home or the domestic environment as the province of the woman and the public arena as the sphere of the man. Louis is expected to handle domestic financial business, while Lestat moves through New Orleans stalking, seducing, and destroying his nightly victims. Lestat reveals no pangs of conscience over his kills, while Louis, despite an irrepressible desire for blood, finds Lestat's tactics in seducing his prey distasteful. Louis has too much compassion for humanity; he insists on feeding only upon rats and other animals. Louis' regret is a constant source of amusement and ridicule for the insensitive, practical-minded Lestat. The traditional gender hierarchy of the domestic unit is sustained within the vampire relationship as well. Lestat manipulates Louis by refusing to provide him with the necessary information to strike out on his own. He intentionally keeps his convert ignorant, refusing to explain their origins and neglecting to tell him whether there are others of their kind. In the context of *Interview*, the reader is led to believe that Lestat simply does not know the answer to these questions. In the second novel, however, the author reveals that Lestat knows more about the source of vampire power than most others do. By keeping Louis ignorant of worldly and philosophical matters, Lestat can ensure his partner's obedience and can keep him dependent. Louis plans to leave only after he decides that Lestat has no information, but Lestat resorts to even more cunning means of maintaining his partner's fidelity.

This portrayal of a same-sex relationship perpetuates one of the most destructive heterosexist myths: the assumption that gay and lesbian domestic units mirror heterosexual unions. Such a thesis is anathema because it prioritizes the heterosexual union, which promises fertility, designating it as normal rather than as merely normative. Such designations then relegate homoeroticism to the unnatural, the demonic inversion of normalcy. As long as same-sex desire is represented as an imperfect replication of the heterosexual union, it will continue to be dismissed as inferior, and the emotional bonds between gay and lesbian couples will be discounted and regarded as misdirected passion—a comic and grotesque parody of the norm. One need only remember that the most common ridicule of the same-sex couple is to inquire which partner is the boy and which is the girl. Moreover, the portrayal of Louis and Lestat's domestic relationship is an example of heterosexist projection. It imposes upon same-sex relations the worst malfunctions of the heterosexual marriage: gender inequity, dominance and submission, spousal abuse, abandonment and neglect, child abuse, etc. Thus, the depiction is in keeping with the current political trend of blaming the decline of the American family upon the single group that is arguably least responsible: those who do not participate in it at all.

After Louis decides to leave Lestat, the latter seeks a new, more potent means of maintaining Louis' loyalty and subservience. A cliché and potentially destructive means of saving a doomed marriage is to strengthen the bond with a child, a mutual creation and a reason to remain together. This is Lestat's solution to his own domestic problems. When Louis discovers Claudia, a small child whose mother has died of yellow fever, he is overcome with maternal compassion and erotic desire. He feeds upon her briefly. Lestat recognizes that he can exploit Louis' affection for this girl. If she is transformed into a vampire, Louis will feel obliged to remain in New Orleans and care for her, and this is indeed what happens. Lestat also suggests that a daughter would constitute a distraction. Indeed, once they are a family, Lestat and Louis become quite domestic, treating Claudia like a child long after she would have been an aged adult. They hire her dressmakers and piano teachers and chastise her when she kills the domestic help, while she throws childish temper tantrums and defies her parents.

The creation of the vampire Claudia is a dark parody of conventional procreation. Both men participate. Louis drains her initially, and Lestat offers her his blood to replenish hers and complete the "dark trick." Louis confesses to Claudia much later: "I took your life ... He gave it back to you" (116). The image of sucking that accompanies the creation of any vampire in the series, of course, signifies infancy. The unique, perverse element of Claudia's conception is that she is the object of desire in the erotic act that constitutes her vampire birth. Thus, the queer family is an erotic triangle (Gelder 113). She spends her first years sleeping in Louis' coffin. Ironically, the family members feed their vampire lust by finding victims for each other. There is even an element of voyeurism insofar as they apparently watch each other during the kill. Louis marvels at the absence of remorse when Lestat and Claudia move in for the kill, and Claudia invites Louis to hunt with her.

Of course, the vampire household is still dysfunctional after Claudia's inclusion. The real trouble begins when Claudia, angry because she can never grow up, inquires about the circumstances of her creation, just as a small child wants to know who made her. A reluctant Louis eventually confesses that he first drank from her. Claudia's incredulous response parallels that of an adult incest survivor: "You fed upon me? ... I was your victim!" (114). Louis blames Lestat for transforming her into a vampire at such an early age, and eventually Claudia also begins to resent Lestat for her predicament, recognizing that both she and Louis are his victims. More and more, the vampire family begins to resemble the abusive household where the mother and the children live in fear of the adult male who refuses to allow them to leave. The typical story has the persecuted members of the household, after long suffering, finally murder the abusive member. Lestat assumes the role of the arrogant, violent father who is indifferent to the suffering of his family. He tells Claudia that he has found someone who would make a much better vampire than her, thus threatening either to abandon his current domestic arrangement or to kill his family members if they do not behave as expected. Claudia and Louis are initially reluctant to leave Lestat because he has convinced them that they need him, that he has information valuable to them. Moreover, Louis believes that the elder vampire would never let them leave because he needs Louis to handle their money. Louis initially manifests battered-wife syndrome. Despite domestic abuse, he still harbors deep affection for, and commitment to, Lestat.

Claudia's aggression toward Lestat is understandable through the Freudian oedipal drama. The vampire's family romance is an utter confusion of gender roles. Although Louis and Lestat are plainly developed as mother and father, Claudia's Electra complex casts them in the opposing roles. The desires of the oedipal girl are initiated by the absence of a penis, a condition for which she blames her mother, who is also bereft of the male organ. As she develops, however, she comes to sympathize and identify with her mother and to long for her father, who possesses the penis that she desires for herself. Claudia's inability to mature into a full-grown woman signifies the infantile condition that Freudian psychology relegates to her (Hodges and Doane 160). The female is regarded as an incomplete male, defined by the absent penis. Claudia resents the father in the same way that the oedipal daughter resents the mother. She blames Lestat for the condition that she regards as inadequate. As a consequence, she allies herself with Louis the mother, desiring his condition and even running off with him as if they were a married couple. It appears that the author has intentionally confused the Freudian psychology within the vampire household, because Claudia also closely resembles the oedipal male child. She develops a longing for the mother and a resentment for the father whom she fears and eventually tries to kill. In this context, her inability to mature might signify her castration by a father who is unwilling to relinquish control over the mother. We find out in the second novel that Lestat resented Claudia's domination of Louis more than he resented her attempt at murder.

Rice may have mixed the male and female oedipal experiences to demonstrate that there are no strict gender categories in immortality. Certainly, Claudia becomes increasingly masculine after she is transformed into a vampire. Louis remarks that she resembles Lestat in the aggressive fashion in which she hunts her victims. The masculinizing of the female vampires seems to be a motif within *The Vampire Chronicles.* Lestat's mother, when transformed into a vampire in the second novel, physically begins to resemble a young boy. Indeed, until *Queen of the Damned,* one could argue that virtually all the vampires are men, regardless of their physical bodies. If Claudia is neither male nor female following her conversion, then it makes sense that her oedipal experience would be confusing. Rice could even be suggesting that relations within the gay family romance produce social or sexual deviants by not exhibiting distinct gender roles.

A rigorous queer reading of the portrayal of Claudia exposes a remarkable homophobia. The creation of Claudia is a gay adoption. She is the child of two men, and her growth has been stunted. The implications of this portrayal are truly hostile to gay parental rights, perpetuating the myth that a child within a same-sex relationship cannot mature in a normative fashion. The parenting of Lestat and Louis serves only to transform Claudia into a sadistic monster. She seduces and destroys humans. One of the most unique features of Rice's vampires is that their human personality traits are immortalized by their vampirism. Claudia's body, frozen in adolescence, mirrors her arrested emotional development. Many years after she would have been an adult, she still displays childlike personality features: intemperate anger, vindictiveness, pouting, tantrums, and sadism. Moreover, the novel plainly indicates that she will never be able to care for herself and will always need the assistance of others. The portrayal of Claudia also seems to affirm the heterosexist fantasy that a child exposed to a gay or lesbian relationship is likely to experience a premature erotic awakening, usually through molestation, and to display a subsequent disposition toward deviant sexuality. Claudia demonstrates an early fascination with maternal figures. She kills the maid and her daughter, whose bodies are found leaning together in a loving embrace. In Paris, fearing abandonment by Louis, she insists that he transform Madeleine, the dollmaker, into a vampire. Of course, Madeleine is to be both mother and lover to Claudia, replacing Louis as her guardian. When the burnt bodies of Claudia and Madeleine are found at the end of the novel, they too are locked in an familial, quasi-erotic embrace.

Homophobic rhetoric has long portrayed the gay and lesbian lifestyle as anathema to order and obligation. In the heterosexist mind, the "choice" of an alternative lifestyle is selfish, the shrugging off of familial obligations. Homosexuals will not produce children, and if they do, they will abandon their offspring in pursuit of each "new hatched, unfledged courage." Although he denies it, Louis is plainly so enamored with Armand that he is, as Claudia observes, likely to abandon her to accompany him. This same situation could also be indicative of the sexist stereotype that men are unable to generate sufficient maternal passion to care adequately for a child.

Returning to the queer household, we must examine the dynamics of the dysfunctional vampire family. The domestic interaction of the undead constitutes an inversion of the ideal family structure. In *The Vampire Chronicles*, the fledgling undead resent and even despise the individual who transformed them. Louis, Nicholas, Gabrielle, and David Talbot all come to resent Lestat. Since we have already concluded that such relationships are erotic and conjugal in nature, it is only a small leap to determine that the vampire marriage is founded upon resentment and hostility. Although Claudia's creation is supposed to improve or at least sustain the relationship between Lestat and Louis, it only serves to delay and later intensify hostilities. Animosities shift from the sparring of Louis and Lestat to the feud between Lestat and Claudia, causing the latter to observe that the family is "locked together in hatred" (116). Indeed, the conflict between Claudia and Lestat degenerates into attempted murder. The situation resembles the justifiable homicide of the domestic tyrant. The vampire family signifies the failed marriage in which the father's abuse prompts the other family members to plot his death. In this cliché domestic situation, the mother or child kills the father and then stirs public sympathy for the victims of domestic violence, sympathy that advocates their right to liberate themselves. Of course, such situations usually involve the father's threat to kill the mother if she tries to leave. Moreover, these domestic disputes stereotypically involve the father's sexual abuse of the children. Claudia's resentment of Lestat derives from the role that he played in her transformation, a sexual assault on a child.

The events immediately preceding and following the attempted murder of Lestat parallel the circumstances of domestic abuse. Louis and Claudia plan to escape from Lestat by sailing to Europe. Louis even attempts to provide financially for his partner before he abandons him; Louis leaves an adequate amount of property in the care of a financial advisor because Lestat is incompetent in such matters. However, Claudia has been secretly planning the murder of Lestat to ensure their safe departure. When she executes her plot, she does it without Louis' endorsement. When the couple arrives in Paris, Louis admits that he would have abandoned Claudia after she attacked Lestat if he thought that she could take care of herself. Louis thus resembles the abused spouse who remains loyal to the sadistic partner despite continual degradation, but who maintains a maternal responsibility toward the abused child despite her actions. The return of Lestat after two attempts to destroy him is reminiscent of the supervillain of television melodramas that portray domestic abuse. The husband doggedly pursues the family to avenge himself for their abandonment. The judgment and punishment of Claudia in the Theatre of the Vampires resembles that aspect of the domestic violence narrative in which the family members are brought to trial and are punished by the patriarchal power structure.

The meeting of Armand and Louis adds an additional dimension to the family drama. Armand signifies the advent of the suitor who competes with the children for the mother's affection. The homoerotic implications of Louis and Armand's flirtation are obvious. Armand offers Louis all that Lestat could or would not. He displays outward affection, offers Louis the knowledge of their origins (indicating that he too has much to learn), rescues Louis from the efforts of the theatre vampires, and accompanies Louis as an equal partner at the end of the novel. Rice fashions Armand as the ideal companion for Louis, one who compensates for all Lestat's flaws. However, his romantic appeal is undermined by the revelation that he perpetrated the attack upon Claudia so Louis would be free of her.

The Freudian implications of Claudia's destruction are complex, and once again they involve a confusion of roles within the family romance. The oedipal drama has broadened by the end of the novel. The reader discovers that Lestat is not dead and that he has returned to execute revenge upon Claudia and win back Louis. His effort to destroy his child signifies the intervention of the father within the mother-infant dyad, which breaks the erotic bond. This action seems gratuitous because Claudia has already found an alternative maternal figure and Louis has found a new partner. The competition for Louis' affection becomes quite complicated, involving three overlapping oedipal triangles: Lestat, Louis, and Claudia; Armand, Louis, and Claudia; and Louis, Madeleine, and Claudia. In each, Claudia constitutes the oedipal child whose maternal bond must be severed. In the first two triangles, Louis is the mother. In the other triangle, his role has shifted to the paternal position. The first two relationships suggest an interesting twist upon Eve Sedgewick's theory of homosocial bonding (21–27). Lestat and Armand compete for Louis' affection by working out their aggression upon a female vampire: Claudia. However, an additional dimension is added to the conflict by the presence of a second female figure: Louis. Armand and Lestat compete to destroy one female while contending to seduce another. Claudia, through her insistence that Madeleine be transformed into a vampire, attempts to escape the wrath of the oedipal fathers by vacating her bond with the oedipal mother. However, Claudia's insistence that Louis transform Madeleine serves to shift his place within the third triangle to the paternal role. He is compelled to create a mother for his child, and when the task is complete, he announces the death of the "last vestige" of his humanity (273). The event masculinizes him. Eventually, he becomes so desensitized that when he learns that Armand perpetrated the destruction of Claudia, the revelation does not even arouse his anger.

The portrayal of the vampire-queer family has profound homophobic implications. The unit is offered as the demonized other of the normative, bourgeois family structure. All of the features of the most hostile domestic environment are projected onto the homoerotic relationship. Most of these features address the fitness of gay or lesbian parents to rear a child. The fluidity of gender destabilizes the domestic environment, offering Claudia no appropriate model for social and erotic behavior. Moreover, the adult vampires can offer her little besides hostility, inconsistency, and indifference. Obviously, such portrayals could be intended to act as comic parodies of the bourgeois family by projecting the commonplace features of the dysfunctional home onto a family of monsters. However, in the contemporary political environment, the creation of a family of inhuman monsters that bears a clear relationship to a gay or lesbian partnership only confirms and reinforces culturally generated prejudices. The right wing already regards gay and lesbian relations as grotesque caricatures of normative familial relationships. In this context, it is easy to misconstrue the nature of the parody. The queer family itself could be the object of a ridicule that parodies the futile efforts of same-sex partners to emulate those social conditions that Western culture has designated as the appropriate conditions for cohabitation.

Here we must move away from our concentration on family politics to address those myths that are commonplace within right-wing, homophobic discourse. Anne Rice's *The Vampire Chronicles* perpetuate many of the most troublesome and hostile stereotypes, even those that have proven most effective in impeding the progress of homosexual demands for social equality. Perhaps the most destructive of all heterosexist delusions involves the association of gays and lesbians with pedophilic desire. This fiction persists despite all evidence to the contrary. The myth is a construction of conservative campaigns to demonize gay males by manipulating the deep fears and anxieties of America's parents for their children. Just as the most volatile racist rhetoric of the civil-rights struggle addressed the anxieties of white society by visualizing the rape of white women by African American males, the family-values discourse of the past decade has created the image of the sodomized child as the ultimate representation of the gay and lesbian menace. This rhetoric has proven effective in stirring the sympathies of a significant segment of the population despite recent academic research that contradicts the claim.

In such a volatile political environment, Rice's portrayal of same-sex desire between adults and adolescents, a passion that seems to lie at the heart of her vision of vampirism, should not escape interrogation. In many ways, her portrayal of pedophilia owes much to the idea of Greek love that is so prevalent in the classics. Erotic relations between an adult male and a prepubescent boy were commonplace, even institutionalized, within Greek society. As Foucault demonstrates in the second volume of his *History of Sexuality*, these relations between men and boys were normative and even served a beneficial educational function. Foucault surveys the archive of Greek texts that debate the priority of same sex relations over heterosexual marriage (*The Care of the Self* 189–232).

In *The Vampire Chronicles*, the structure of undead relations is by nature pedophilic. The conversion process involves the meeting of an ancient vampire and a much younger human. The relationship is necessarily educational because the fledgling vampire desires to understand his condition and considers the older vampire the obvious source of valuable information. Even in cases where the vampire transforms an adult human, that person can still be regarded as a child to immortality, a condition characterized by ignorance, awe, and wonder. In *Interview*, Lestat subverts this tradition by refusing to provide his partners with any of the details that would dispel the air of mystery around their lives. He will not even tell them whether there are others like them. Louis and Claudia must search for others once they are free of the older vampire's tyranny. A similar dearth of knowledge characterized Lestat's own conversion. He is abducted by Magnus, who teaches him only enough to survive before the elder vampire destroys himself. While the absence of information about eternity could be construed as the nature of the human condition, the reader of Rice's novel is led to believe that the vampires actually have the information but refuse to dispense it because the ignorance of the fledgling serves to increase the dominant vampire's control. In the Greek pederastic tradition, the relations did not take place between members of the same social rank. The dominant male was of a higher status than his love object. Often, the object of desire was a household slave.

The examples of eroticism between adults and children within *The Vampire Chronicles* are numerous. The vampires' hunger for human flesh is lascivious in nature and is particularly inflamed by the innocence and tenderness of children. The frame of *Interview* is a case in point. Louis' confessions are made to an unnamed "boy" who, at the end of the novel, begs to be made into a vampire. Louis, angered that the interviewer has missed the whole point of his lengthy narrative, chooses only to frighten him. When Louis first encounters Claudia in the plague-infested section of New Orleans, his attraction to her is erotic. Although attacking humans is against his principles, he is aroused and overwhelmed by her beauty, helplessness, and innocence. Lestat has the most consistent appetite for youthful flesh. Louis explains that "a fresh young girl" was his partner's "favorite food," but that Lestat's greatest triumph was a "young man" about the same age as the interviewer (41). While they live on Louis' plantation, Lestat's most noteworthy kill is the Freniere boy, whose family is devastated by the loss and whose sister Louis tries to help. Later, Lestat begins to woo a young musician in New Orleans, who is also described as a boy. Louis indicates that Lestat's flirtation with the musician went on much longer than any other. Eventually, Louis notices puncture wounds on the boy's neck. The flirtation suggests a long erotic courtship that results in the boy's conversion. Perhaps the most blatant representation of pedophilia in the first novel is the young boy whom Armand presents to Louis in the Theatre of the Vampires. Each vampire gets only a small taste of the boy who offers himself to Louis in a highly erotic fashion:

> He was offering it to me. He was pressing the length of his
> body against me now and I felt the hard strength of his sex
> beneath his clothes pressing against my clothes [230].

The vampire briefly drinks from the yielding boy, and both individuals experience deep ecstasy. The vampire culture has its rules about encounters between adults and children. Although there is no prohibition against feeding on mortal children and such encounters are even desirable, the vampires are warned not to transform a child into a member of the undead. In *The Vampire Lestat*, the titular character is advised never to create a vampire as young as Armand, who is described as boyish. Because the second novel is mostly a prequel to *Interview*, the reader realizes that Lestat consciously violated the prohibition against child vampires when he converted Claudia. It could be argued that this breach of the taboo constitutes his tragic flaw. When Claudia attempts to destroy him, she first does so by offering him two dead children who, she explains, are drunk on "a thimble full" of wine. Claudia's ploy constitutes a symbolic restitution for her suffering. She tries to destroy Lestat through the pedophilic longings that resulted in her own predicament. When Lestat recognizes that he has been poisoned, Claudia asks: "Don't you like the taste of children's blood?" (136).

The interdiction against pedophilia is partially derived from the assumption that exposure to sex at an early age has an enduring, negative impact upon a child's emotional development. Certainly, Claudia's early introduction to vampirism affects her. She becomes a child monster who has no control over her sexual hunger. She kills indiscriminately without observing the appropriate precautions that are intended to save the vampires from discovery. Moreover, her hunting techniques are related to her condition as an immortal. She exploits her appearance by pretending to be lost and frightened, and when mortals attempt to assist her, she kills them. The victims of child abuse claim that the experience has permanently influenced their character, affecting their ability to mature emotionally and their willingness to trust others. They become hostile and vindictive toward the people whom they consider responsible for their condition. Claudia blames Lestat for her unhappiness. Although at first she appears to forgive Louis for his participation in her creation, her resentment comes out at the end of the novel when she fears that he will abandon her for Armand. To compel Louis to perform the "dark trick" upon Madeleine, Claudia reveals her true sentiments: "Do you know that I despise you with a passion that eats at me like a canker?" (261). Once Louis complies, she becomes friendly again. She wears her vulnerability like a suit of armor, using every emotion in her personal arsenal, including self-pity. Armand was also created too early in his emotional development. The master painter, Marius, was waiting for the boy to mature fully before he transformed Armand into an immortal: "Soon, my darling, my love, my little one, when you're strong enough and tall enough, and there is no flaw in you anymore" (*Lestat* 294). Armand is not yet "ready for the burden" of immortality (*Lestat* 295). Armand's neediness is the sign of his immaturity. He seduces both Louis and Lestat in their respective chronicles, hoping that the vampires can restore his joy in life by acquainting him with the changing world from which he has become alienated.

Where there is a prohibition, there is a desire. A society does not generate laws regulating behavior that people would never manifest. Thus, the strong prohibition against sex with children reveals a deep, repressed longing that some are unable to resist. The vampires experience a powerful desire for children's flesh. In relationship to the queer reading of the novel, such portrayals are extremely destructive because they reinforce the myth that gays and lesbians prey upon children, who are intellectually weak and unable to resist temptation or physical threat. Although the novels suggest that the vampire group imposes social prohibitions against such behavior, the novels also suggest that those prohibitions are frequently unsuccessful. Such portrayals prove remarkably destructive because parents' fears for their children lie at the heart of homophobia. Militant homophobes have appropriated this fiction to mobilize public outrage against homosexuals. Countless examples of child molestation go unacknowledged within the confines of the family unit; these generally involve the abuse of a young girl by her father. Yet the infrequent examples of sexual abuse among young boys by a gay man create public scandals replete with death threats and lynch mobs. Perhaps this phenomenon can be attributed to traditional sexism, wherein a young female is already regarded as an object of desire so her mistreatment is considered less outrageous than the molestation of a boy. The issue can also be related to heterosexism. The abuse of the girl is at least a preamble to normative sexual relations, while the abuse of a boy is generally an introduction to deviant lifestyles (Califia 62–63). The equation of gays and lesbians to pedophiles is contrary to fact. Queer readers should not let it go unchallenged.

The association of gays and lesbians with predatory sexual behavior and promiscuity serves to consolidate homophobic sentiment among members of the mainstream public. Gender stereotyping has coded homosexuals, particularly gay males, as desperate for sexual stimulation from a seemingly endless variety of partners. However, this myth particularly emphasizes the paranoid fantasies of heterosexual males who assume that they are the target of an aggressive sexuality that threatens to undermine their virility or reputation. They fear an aggressive sexuality that has the power to seduce. The sexuality is at once the same and the other. While gender stereotypes characterize gay males as effeminate and implicitly passive, they also postulate an enterprising sexuality that regards all male heterosexuals as objects of desire to be pursued vigorously. In the past decade, the association of queers with predatory eroticism and promiscuity has proven particularly potent in rallying public sentiment against homosexuals, particularly since the AIDS crisis was, and still is, fallaciously blamed on gay promiscuity (Treichler 65). Thus, the heterosexual population insulated itself against fear of exposure by presuming that homosexuals had invited catastrophe through a reckless lifestyle. In Rice's novels, the equation of gays and lesbians with vampires serves to validate this destructive, homophobic fiction. The vampires are portrayed both as predators and as parasites who are dependent upon the mortal population to sustain them. Their immortality is little more than an endless succession of indiscriminate erotic encounters in which they attempt to slake an unquenchable thirst for blood. Each night, all night, they seek new victims, never returning to the same person twice.

Guilt stricken, Louis feeds upon animals, which mirrors the typical diet of humanity, while Lestat seeks humans, "sometimes two or three a night, sometimes more" (41). Lestat characterizes their lives as "rich feasts that conscience cannot appreciate and mortal men cannot know without regret." He continues, "God kills, and so shall we; indiscriminately" (88). Lestat's argument for promiscuity concedes that their behavior is a violation of normative principles of restraint. Liberation from sexual restraint and the pangs of conscience is the principal advantage of vampirism.

The heterosexist distortion of queer behavior includes myths about the proliferation of homosexuality; these are, of course, derived from the accusations of predatory eroticism. Conservatives paradoxically characterize one partner in a queer tryst as a homosexual and the other as a victim of that homosexual. The heterosexist maintains that all homosexuals are created by other homosexuals, meaning that all queers are converts, ruined heterosexuals. The alternative lifestyle is a paradox for many of its detractors. On the one hand, it is frequently conceptualized as nothing more than a series of poor choices and deviant behaviors made by an otherwise normal person. On the other hand, the homosexual is an identifiable individual who manifests predictable physical characteristics and inevitable behavioral patterns. Thus, the homosexual does and does not exist. sometimes he is a person and sometimes he is merely a practice. Conservative theorists postulate the existence of the heterosexual, but they do not acknowledge the opposing category that makes this definition meaningful. This assumption serves to invalidate homoerotic passion, fashioning it as a fabrication, a learned sentiment that no one really feels. Thus, the motivation to become a homosexual is exterior and not interior. Gays and lesbians are not people, but they are a body of knowledge that is passed on from one convert to another. This assumption results in the myth of "recruitment," the belief that gays and lesbians share the heterosexual desire to perpetuate themselves, to have children. The only way to do so is to recruit new members from the heterosexual population. Of course, the myth holds that the most efficient means of enlisting new homosexuals is to prey upon children, who are more vulnerable and less likely to repel temptation.

Rice's queer vampires are certainly engaged in recruitment. The only way the undead can increase is by manufacturing more undead through the process that Rice has titled the "dark trick." It is interesting that in archaic gay slang, the word "trick" means a sexual conquest, particularly a one-night stand. No vampire is born a vampire. Every vampire is converted through a forced encounter, a rape. All vampire encounters include unwilling participants, some of whom also become vampires. In addition, these erotic moments are generally destructive to the human victim, who either dies or is permanently transformed. This explains the resentment of the vampires toward those individuals who create them. They blame the parent vampire both for interrupting the normal course of their lives and for introducing them to a life of continual ecstasy without dynamics, which is a sterile and pointless existence. Louis is determined never to make another vampire. When he is compelled to do so by Claudia, it is only out of guilt at having participated in her transformation and ruination. When the boy interviewer begs to be made into a vampire at the end of the narrative, he inspires Louis' anger and not his admiration or passion. The myth that gays and lesbians wish to convert the heterosexual population, particularly children, has proven to be a potent tool in the slander and mischaracterization of alternative sexual identities. In the temporarily successful campaign for Amendment Two in Colorado, homophobes' fear of the recruitment of children was cited as one of the primary motivations for the project.

Louis' disposition leads to the next inaccurate characterization of gay and lesbian subjectivity: the heterocentric presumption that all queers are unhappy because they do not get to enjoy life's periodic rituals and celebrations. Queers and vampires do not marry and have children, the events commonly regarded as the height of human aspiration and happiness. The confessional structure of *Interview* goes a long way to validating the fallacious assumption of gay guilt and melancholy. Louis tells the story of his life to articulate his misery: the burden that is immortality. His anger at the interviewer stems from the boy's failure to grasp the thesis of the narrative. None of the vampires in Rice's first novel seem well adjusted. Louis and Lestat constitute a dichotomy between two extreme positions. Louis' melancholy borders on the suicidal, and Lestat's callousness is pathological. Lestat plays the spinet while his father dies. He seduces and kills without compunction. Louis, on the other hand, is all regret, refusing to accept his vampire compulsion to feed upon humanity. The portrayal suggests that gays are either detached and remorseless or regretful and penitent. Claudia, as indicated before, is also unhappy about her condition. She is furious over her lost humanity at the same time that she revels in the blood feast. Armand desires companionship because he believes that Louis can reintroduce him to a world that has lost its allure through centuries of tedious ecstacy. Armand explains that very few vampires have the stamina for eternity. Eventually all of the earthly pleasures that made that individual desire immortality pass, and the vampire no longer has a desire to live in an alien world. The undead must make a concerted effort to adapt to each passing milieu. Thus, Armand desires Louis' company, believing that Louis can acquaint him with the very spirit of the new age. From *The Vampire Lestat*, the reader learns that most vampires, after the length of a few human life spans, practice self-immolation by walking into fire, an idea that expands the stereotypes to include queer suicide and invites intervention. The emotional evolution of the vampires involves a movement toward indifference and numbness. Eventually, Louis is as dispassionate as Lestat. He destroys the Theatre of the Vampires in retaliation for the murder of Claudia, but at the end of the novel when he discovers Armand's complicity in the attack, he is unable to experience rage or resentment. This movement suggests that homosexuals eventually become incapable of sentiment and commitment.

Another common facet of the gay-melancholia myth is the presumption that given the opportunity for conversion, all homosexuals would prefer to be straight. This heterocentric supposition fortifies the belief that homosexuality constitutes a deviation from a normative psychological development. It states that had life gone well for the individual in her formative years, she would have chosen a socially sanctioned lifestyle. The queer reading of Rice's vampires certainly bolsters the deviation narrative. Most of the undead long to be human again, acknowledging that a few brief years of dynamic life are superior to the monotony of eternity. Lestat believes that all humans desire to be vampires and that all vampires long to be human again. However, in *The Tale of the Body Thief*, Lestat is given the opportunity to exchange bodies with a human. After lengthy consideration and the rebuke of everyone to whom he broaches the idea, he decides to experiment. Of course, Raglan James, the man with the capacity to carry out the exchange, absconds with Lestat's body leaving him powerless in an alien form. Much of Lestat's experience in the novel is intended to demonstrate the stinking, cumbersome vulgarity of the human frame as compared to the vampire's body. He is repulsed by the stench of bodily functions and is dissatisfied with human physical limitations. When Lestat becomes human, one of his first actions is to copulate with a woman; he deflowers a nun, a particularly irreverent act. This event is immediately followed by his attempted seduction of David Talbot, who confesses that he is inclined toward same-sex passion and that he finds Lestat's new body very desirable. Nevertheless, he elects to show restraint. Lestat acknowledges that even before his initial conversion to vampirism, he desired both men and women. Lestat's desperate attempt to steal his own body reveals the extent to which he has rejected this compulsion to be human despite its many allures. The inclusion of W. B. Yeats' poem "Sailing to Byzantium" at the beginning of *Tale* reinforces the novel's repudiation of the flesh. The poem's speaker pleads to be gathered "into the artifice of eternity," maintaining that "Once out of nature … [he] shall never take/… [his] bodily form from any natural thing."

Homosexual anxiety has still another manifestation in *The Vampire Chronicles*. The religious imagery invokes the heterosexist preoccupation with the salvation of homosexuals. The vampire's search for meaning and origin can be construed as a religious quest, buttressing the homophobic presumption that all queers are guilt ridden, preoccupied, and incapacitated by the desire to make their lives suitable to God's hetero/phallocentric will. The beauty of the first novel is that the knowledge of origins is unattainable for the vampire, even in eternity. The spiritual condition of the undead is similar to humanity's. Even in undeath, there is no revelation. Indeed, Rice's novel *Memnoch the Devil* constitutes the completion of the spiritual quest for many of the vampires yearning for enlightenment and for a confirmation of divinity. Louis conceives of his reiterated crimes in religious terms. Following the presumed murder of Lestat, Louis experiences a religious ecstasy, one that reveals the absence of God from the world's cathedrals and his own similarity to Cain, who murdered his brother and who must now wander the earth. In *The Vampire Lestat*, the undead are highly superstitious, believing themselves outcasts from grace and the church. Like the conversion narrative, this reading of the homophobic allegory within the novel is eventually recuperated by Lestat. Armand's band of vampires, who live in the Parisian cemetery, have been conditioned to believe that they are forbidden to intrude upon God's sanctuary: "[W]e don't belong in the house of God" (*Lestat* 190). Lestat is successful in dispelling the prohibition about entering the church. Although his presumption at first makes him the focus of the other vampires' scorn, he eventually convinces them that their fears are unfounded.

Religion operates as social control among the vampires. As long as the undead believe that they are beyond the pale of salvation, they remain subdued, observing the hierarchy of power and accepting their own repression and humility. This episode is particularly meaningful for the queer reader because the religious rhetoric of the past twenty years has sought to exclude homosexuals from salvation and to convince them that they should not strive for equality because they are denounced in a document that was written thousands of years ago. Indeed, the religious community seems to be obsessed with the salvation of homosexuals. The opposition to the gay-rights movement is invariably articulated in explicitly religious terminology that suggests that gays and lesbians do not deserve civil rights because they fail to comply with religious strictures. In *Memnoch the Devil*, where both God and the devil struggle for Lestat's allegiances and where God's righteousness is not assumed, Rice obscures the metaphysical and moral position of the vampires, obliterating the previously constructed dichotomy between the saved and the damned that is so commonplace in the cultural dispute of sexual politics.

Throughout *The Vampire Chronicles*, the undead are associated with aristocratic decadence and high art. In his book, *The Wilde Century*, Alan Sinfield argues that the stereotypical links among homosexuality, aristocracy, aestheticism, and effeminacy have their origins in the trails of Oscar Wilde in the last decade of the nineteenth century (11–12). The suggestion that gays and lesbians are the fountainhead of the arts is problematic because it leads to the related assumption that homosexuals control the arts, thus fueling much of the right-wing demagoguery and hostility toward the humanities. Following the 1996 "Republican revolution," the first objects of scrutiny were the National Endowment of the Arts and the humanities.

Rice's vampires are highly cultured. The vampire family maintains its box at the Theatre d'Orleans, the new French opera house, and Louis tries to instill in Claudia an appreciation for the arts, encouraging her to read poetry and to pursue her skills at the piano. Lestat chooses a musician as a companion after his relationship with Louis and Claudia begins to sour. After Claudia and Louis arrive in Paris, they discover that the local vampires are operating a theater. The association of the revenants with drama perpetuates the clichés that the theater is largely comprised of homosexuals and that gays are successful at dramatics because they are highly emotional. The subterranean ballroom in which the Theatre of the Vampires' residents live is lavishly decorated with some of Western art's most ghastly and vivid masterpieces:

> I could see a world of frescoes and murals surrounded us, their colors deep and vibrant above the dancing flame, and gradually the theme and content beside us came clear. It was the terrible *Triumph of Death* by Brueghel, painted on such a massive scale that all the multitude of ghastly figures towered over us in the gloom [*Interview* 227–28].

Also included are Hieronymus Bosch's *Garden of Earthly Delights* and Durer's *Four Horsemen*. In *The Vampire Lestat*, Marius was a successful Renaissance artist whose work adorned the walls of churches and chapels, and Armand was his favorite model. Before his transformation, Lestat was a player in a Parisian theater, and his friend Nicholas was a violinist. Nicholas later becomes the tortured vampire playwright of the Theatre of the Vampires, where he creates a variety of grotesque masterpieces.

The link between vampires and art has another manifestation. The undead themselves signify art. Like Keats' Grecian urn, they remain unchanged throughout the centuries, signifying the desire for permanence in a world fraught with grief and mutability. Louis, walking in the Louvre, admires the representations of the human will, which triumphs over death. Just like the visual representations on Keats' urn, the vampires signify the joys of life suspended at a moment of peak intensity, an ecstasy that is both lifeless and full of life. The vampires are preserved in a realm of continual, ecstatic stimulation that becomes monotonous through eternal repetition. Keats laments that the trees will never throw down their leaves, the lovers will never kiss, and the flautist will never stop playing his song. Thus, "Ode to a Grecian Urn" arrives at the same conclusion as *Interview*, arguing that a few years of pleasure in which a finite number of intense joys, which are made more valuable by the certainty of grief and pain, is superior to an eternity in which little or nothing ever changes. The vampires become tired of their existence because their lives are an uninterrupted ecstasy of blood. Keats concludes that he prefers the vicissitudes of human life to the inactivity of eternity. However, the allusions to Yeats' "Sailing to Byzantium" in *The Tale of the Body Thief* reverses the sentiments expressed in *Interview*. Yeats concludes that the "artifice of eternity" is superior to the "dying animal." Lestat decides that the eternity of vampirism is superior to the vulgarity and the limitations of mortality. Rice's vampires are themselves artistic creations suspended on the pages of multiple novels, celebrating and interrogating humanity's long-ing for immortality.

The aristocratic leisure of the undead invokes the stereotypes of luxury, decadence, idleness, and effeminacy that are a major part of the dominant culture's homophobic fiction. The image of Louis and Lestat living on a plantation at the beginning of *Interview* and feeding on the slaves invokes a Marxist thematic that is difficult to ignore. The aristo-cratic vampires are "defined by excess and unrestrained appetite" (Gelder 22). Their power grows as they consume more and more people. Even in the city, Louis and Lestat have servants whom they ultimately destroy. Moreover, the vampires never work in the space of four novels. Lawyers and brokers handle the vampires' money, leaving them free to pursue less tedious, more pleasurable tasks. They sleep all day and indulge in the pleasures of the flesh all night. Lestat's victimization of children may be the plainest representation of the vampire's aristocratic callousness and decadence. Armand's mortal boy is treated like a fine wine; everyone gets a small taste of a treat too delicate to squander. Even the vampire chil-dren are monsters of sensuality and consumption. When an uprising of slaves drives Lestat and Louis from the plantation, they move to New Orleans, where they can be less conspicuous, thus subtly invoking the cliché that gays and lesbians migrate to the city for culture and anonymity. Louis praises all that Paris has to offer, suggesting that it is the source of sophistication and high culture: "[I]f the world outside here were to sink into darkness, what was fine, what was beautiful, what was essential might there still come to its finest flower" (*Interview* 204).

The aristocratic lifestyle traditionally carries the mark of effeminacy. Considered in light of outdated gender constructs, the novel contains many more examples of vampire effeminacy than would be evident from a contemporary view. The classical and the early modern points of view coded unrestrained sensuality as feminine. The Enlightenment, with its emphasis on bourgeois values of labor and materialism, regarded idleness as effeminate. In *Interview*, the vampires are described as dandies, "richly dressed and gracefully walking through the pools of light" (40). They attract no notice because New Orleans is full of "exotic creatures" (40). When Louis first encounters Santiago in the streets of Paris, both vam-pires, dressed in coat and capes, are the image of urban sophistication and effeminate gentility.

In a society whose principal value is materialism, one might wonder what is so offensive about the image of rich, leisure class homosexuals who enjoy their wealth and freedom. In the context of contemporary sexual politics, such portrayals prove detrimental to the advance of gay rights.

Conservatives mischaracterize gays and lesbians as a privileged class to undermine the struggle for equality. By suggesting that the group already has more than its share of the wealth, they disassociate homosexuals from the middle-class value of hard work. The dominant culture fictionalizes the image of gays and lesbians to construct the group as a deviant threat to mainstream values. The political rhetoric of the 1992 presidential campaign reveals this process at work. Republicans attacked a group that they termed the "cultured elite," arguing that too much of American entertainment is geared toward a class of privileged individuals. Gays and lesbians are frequently included in this group because of the predictable association between homosexuality and the arts. Other groups included within the broad, ill-defined "cultured elite" were academics, who are frequently too liberal to vote Republican, and traditionally associated with gentility, isolation, and high ideas, and Hollywood, whose work is regarded as decadent and, despite clear evidence, unacceptable to the working class.

The novel also seems to endorse the closet for homosexuals. The vampires live in fear of discovery by their servants or their neighbors, and the plantation uprising is an example of the consequences that follow the revelation of the vampires' true natures. The coffin is the closet; the vampires only come out at night when they are less conspicuous. Their secretive lives signify the necessity that queers remain silent and invisible. Just as homosexuals remain in the closet to avoid violence and persecution, the vampires fear destruction if discovered. They are the vulnerable predators who feed upon others until discovery, at which time they flee for their lives. They form secret societies where they can socialize, but they remain separate from mainstream society. In *Queen of the Damned*, the undead meet in secret in the backrooms of nightclubs. The third novel could be construed as a coming-out story. Lestat becomes a high-profile figure, a rock star who sings about his life as a vampire. From this perspective, the anger and resentment that he inspires suggests that gays repress each other, policing their own closets and expecting others to maintain the silence. The other vampires seek to kill Lestat for making their lives public. This theme diverts attention away from the real cause of queer invisibility: culturally imposed silence and legal persecution.

The inevitable topic that follows any mention of gay males, particularly when blood is involved, is AIDS. Certainly, the topic would be anachronistic in *Interview* because the novel predates the pandemic. However, the issues addressed in this chapter are heterotextuality and queer reading. One can only read in the present social context, where any discussion of homosexuality becomes a discourse about AIDS. The synthesis of vampirism and homosexuality perpetuates the stereotypical link between homoeroticism, disease, and death. It continues to shape and define gay males as walking afflictions. Ellis Hanson has detailed the parallel signification of vampirism and AIDS in his article "Undead." AIDS has provided right-wing extremists with the pretext for persecution that was lost when the American Psychiatric Association determined that homosexuality is not a pathology. Conservatives created a new reason to denounce same-sex relations as unnatural and unhealthy (Bayer 202). I do not only refer to the religious hysterics' myth of origin for the pandemic (i.e., God's wrath), an explanation that was and is particularly mystifying when one considers that lesbians are the social group least likely to contract the disease. Another explanation sought to blame gay promiscuity for the epidemic. Some initial reports translated gay men into sexual supermen capable of 30 to 40 sexual encounters a night. In the rush to make the sick responsible for their own suffering, no one even considered whether such heroic sexual athletics were even physically possible (Treichler 46).

The parallel between AIDS and vampirism generates abundant significations. The vampires are literally suspended between life and death; they are revenants, walking corpses. Paradoxically, the vampires do not fear impending death, but instead the knowledge that they may never die burdens them. An erotic encounter with one of the vampires either kills immediately or produces another walking carcass. Of course the exchange of blood creates the revenants. Perhaps the vampire's immortality is a metaphor for the often lengthy, agonizing period in which the infected individual remains healthy, spreading death to all her partners. Rice's vampires often impersonate death. Armand plays the grim reaper in his performance at the Theatre of the Vampires, and most of the plays that Nicholas writes in *The Vampire Lestat* represent vampirism as a danse macabre. In the narrative of his life, Armand relates vampirism to the bubonic plague: "[W]e were to be as the Black Death itself, a vexation without explanation, to cause man to doubt the mercy and intervention of God" (*Lestat* 301). The images of the vampires' appearances are reminiscent of what is called "wasting" in the final stages of AIDS. The vampires are pale, thin, and gaunt with the gentility and elegance that accompanies long suffering. In this context, the third novel, *Queen of the Damned*, becomes a representation of pandemic. This novel was written after the advent of the disease. Akasha, the mother of all vampires, awakes and spreads death to all of her progeny. *The Tale of the Body Thief* then signifies the desire to escape the afflicted body.

Here the politics of queer reading prove atavistic, erasing the past two decades of social activism. The comparison between the pandemic and vampirism reinforces many repugnant stereotypes about HIV victims. It perpetuates the portrayal of AIDS victims who have no control over their lives and who indiscriminately spread death to the innocent. The predacious sexuality of the AIDS vampire poses a threat to the general population. Thus, the characterization prolongs the homophobic opposition between those who are at risk and those who are not, those who deserve to have the disease and those who do not, those who are deceivers and those who are deceived. The vampires' unrestrained sexuality reinforces the spurious legend of the vindictive, unprincipled homosexual who consciously spreads the disease to his sexual partners out of resentment for his own condition.

Rice's vampire novels advance some sexist and heterosexist notions of the origins of male homosexuality. The characters search for their genesis in Europe and the Middle East. Their inability to explain their own existence torments them. Lestat cautions Louis that they must "live with the knowledge that there is no knowledge" (120). The reader does, however, discover in the second novel that vampires do have a specific ancestry and are one large family, extending back to an Egyptian queen named Akasha, who awakens at the end of the second novel in *The Vampire Chronicles* and kills her husband, Enkil. In *Queen of the Damned*, the reader learns that her intention is to destroy most of the world's males to establish matriarchy and thereby eliminate violence. Her action is paradoxical since she resorts to apocalyptic violence to rid the world of aggression. In the final chapters of the third novel, the conflict revolves around two mothers struggling for dominance. Akasha is the castrating, husband-killing mother who is aggressive and dominant, and Maharet is the obsessively nurturing mother who has lovingly tracked the progress of her family for over 4,000 years. Each of these maternal figures offers its own spurious theory of the genesis of homosexuality. Akasha suggests that the overly dominant, controlling mother is at fault. Maharet signifies the maternal bond that is never sufficiently breached, resulting in the male child's identification with the mother rather than with the father. Both of these theories are sexist because they invest the woman with complete responsibility for the child's sexuality, particularly if the child develops an alternative sexual identity. Moreover, they seem to confirm the Freudian theory that gays and lesbians have been arrested emotionally at some point prior to sexual maturity, thus implying once again that homosexuals are ruined heterosexuals who are by nature histrionic and infantile. The result of these fictions is the continued paternalism that results in pseudophilanthropic gestures, concealing repression under a veil of concern and treatment.

The sexuality of the vampires seems to be of a particularly feminine eroticism. I refer to more than the imagery of sucking that is an inherent part of every vampire myth. Freud defined women's sexuality as a lacking. Because the woman has no penis, she is forever seeking one from men, hence her desire. Rice's vampires are coded in very much the same way. The author has taken great pains to suggest that the longing of the vampire for human flesh is the longing for something that has been lost in their conversion. The act perhaps suggests a desire to be human again. In the first novel, Claudia explains her desire:

> I kill humans every night. I seduce them, draw them close
> to me with an insatiable hunger, a constant never-ending
> search for something ... something, I don't know what it is
> [*Interview* 124].

Lestat, coaching Louis, characterizes the kill as an "experience of another life," and Louis counters with the observation that it is like "that loss of ... [his] own life" (29). The vampires' eroticism is an attempt to relive the ecstatic moment of their transformation, the encounter in which they were the phallic object of a vampire's desire. The Freudian account of female sexuality is phallocentric, defining women as incomplete males. In the context of these novels, it codes homosexuals as incomplete men. In the case of gay sexual identity, the use of the Freudian model of women's eroticism misrepresents the variety of gender roles that are a part of the gay subjectivity. The gay male is, therefore, always a woman in bed, thus advancing reductionist heterosexist logic.

I will now examine how the heterotextual implications of *The Vampire Chronicles* are recuperated so that I do not suggest that Anne Rice is a homophobe. One aspect of the novels that has been ignored in the course of this discussion is the reader's identification with the vampires. It is obvious that Rice wanted the audience to relate to Louis in the first novel and to Lestat in those that follow. After all, the vampires are usually the only characters who are fully drawn. She has added something new to vampire fiction by making the undead the protagonists. However, when the reader identifies with Louis, what is she endorsing? Louis is tortured by self-doubt and the desire to escape his vampire nature, and Lestat, the individual who accepts his nature, is the antagonist in the first novel. Is the audience invited to find Louis appealing only because he finds himself in an untenable position about which he can do nothing? Of course, this observation does not account for the other three novels in which Lestat is the focus, except insofar as his character is made much more appealing when he becomes the narrator. *The Vampire Lestat* begins with a repudiation of Louis' characterization of his partner. In other words, Lestat indicates that Louis is a liar. Rice had to make him more attractive if she wanted him to be heroic and sympathetic.

The space between the two representations of Lestat would seem to be the public space of condemnation that forces capitulation on the part of gays, lesbians, and their supporters before it permits a successful public articulation of queer ideas. The text has to achieve a compromise with the dominant fiction. Although the novels breach the culturally imposed silence upon the issue of homosexuality, they are still engaged in a negotiation with the power structure to compromise the positive portrayal of homosexuals in favor of one that is more socially palatable, one that has the potential for mainstream success. So queers can be represented in the context of the popular fiction as long as all the correct markers are included to inform the reader that the behavior of the characters is not to be emulated; it is not normative. Thus, the moral reader can be led to the socially and historically constituted notion of normative sexuality by the demonized representation of the queer vampires whose lives are wretched and undesirable. The vampires may evoke pity or sympathy, but they do not invite empathy, except perhaps from the queer reader. Moreover, pity and sympathy are operative in the maintenance of the heterosexist social hierarchy, as illustrated when Ralph Reed told his Christian Coalition (the source of most homosexual repression in America) that queers deserve their "sympathy and prayers."

Anne Rice's portrayal of queer vampires could be intended for another purpose. The queer family in *Interview* could be an intentional parody of the normative family, intended to create an irreverent bourgeois horror story. If the intention of horror fiction is to frighten, it is probable that the people whom Rice intended to spook are the heterosexist, middle-class people who regard homosexuality as an insidious threat to the family politics and as a danger to the normative sexual development of their children. Thus the queer family becomes a camp parody, a flaunting of all that is most frightening about the homosexual menace. In this reading, Rice's objective would be to scandalize and to challenge the moralism of the bourgeoisie. Certainly her pornography is a testament to her willingness to undertake such a project.

The identification of the reader with the vampires does not produce a queer reading of the novels. The heterosexual reader is not forced to accept a homocentric eroticism to enjoy the novels. The vampires are not human; they do not have sex. They experience something approximating sex, perhaps a metaphor for sex. Thus, Rice has created something unique.

She has created a homoerotic sexuality, and yet she has reduced the opportunity for social condemnation and increased the market potential of such a subject matter. She has accomplished this by suspending her characters in a world where normative notions of sexual propriety do not apply. If the desire to alienate the middle class were her project, one would have to declare that project a failure. One cannot achieve as broad a success as Anne Rice has without appealing to the middle class. However, she may be attempting to hoodwink her bourgeois readers, offering them an unrestrained sexuality in a form that exposes the hypocrisy of the dominant sexual ideology. By endorsing queer eroticism in a marginalized subjectivity that is not policed by the rules governing sexual exchange, the heterosexist reader acknowledges that gender roles are not nature, but culture.

I do not want to leave my own examination of the homophobic implications of Rice's work unexamined. I must acknowledge that there is something to be said about a study that meticulously catalogs every potentially offensive detail of a novel and, in some cases, may even produce the offending representation. Such a study may even do more damage than the novel itself by exposing those features of the text that may have gone undetected by a less sensitive, guarded reader. One might argue as well that in repudiating every feature of the stereotypical homosexual, I am revealing a profound homophobia that cannot, and dare not, look upon a revelation of the self. Such a reading could also be construed as capitulationist, an attempt to remove all that is unique about queer culture to represent gays and lesbians as middle class and, therefore, inoffensive. Such a reading seeks to earn the trust of the dominant culture and to gain social equality at the expense of true diversity. Such a agenda would legitimize the bourgeois claim to cultural supremacy and endorse the project of repression against all those who do not conform. My denial of the traditional stereotypes is an effort to repudiate the heterosexist assumption that the above features are universal within queer subjectivity and that the behavior of homosexuals can be predicted, and even modified, on the basis of information that defines only a very limited population within the gay community. The reading is not intended to make queers more palatable or even to suggest that the stereotypes repudiated here are never descriptive. The reading seeks to undermine the oversimplification of queer identity and to expose the contradictions that lie at the heart of myth.

Chapter 2

ENGENDERING WHITENESS: THE POLITICS OF RACE, GENDER, AND CLASS IN *THE FEAST OF ALL SAINTS*

In her study entitled *Whiteness Visible*, Valerie Babb exposes the constructedness of racial ideology in America, revealing that the category white does not signify either a biological reality or a transhistorical cultural unity (9). She argues that the concept of whiteness in America was generated to forge a unified national identity among diverse groups of European settlers who had formerly no sense of commonality and who may have even harbored ancient animosities and ethnic grudges while still in their homelands (37). Moreover, this social, pseudoscientific category evolved in opposition to the burgeoning African American community that was perceived as alien and even threatening to those of European descent (14–15). Increasingly, the idea of whiteness came to signify a "system of privileges accorded to people with white skin" (9) or a "means through which certain individuals are granted greater degrees of social acceptance and access" (3). Thus, the concept of whiteness became virtually indistinguishable from the concept of patriarchy. Because women were treated as nonentities in both systems, whiteness and patriarchy, both categories came to represent the power and privilege of men, explicitly white men.

Such an argument is particularly appropriate for a discussion of *The Feast of All Saints* because in her second novel, Anne Rice deconstructs racial classification, demonstrating the permeable nature of the racial designations that our culture perceives as natural and immutable. In Rice's novel, the social practice that is responsible for the constant puncturing of the fictional racial divide is the reciprocal exchange of wealth and sex, or placage, a pseudomarital and quasi-respectable arrangement between a white male and a woman of African or mixed descent. The rich, white male would offer financial support for the resulting family in exchange for sexual favors (Kinlaw and Kasee 216). The result of these liaisons was a culture of mixed-race people, the *gens de couleur libre*, who occupied a middle space between the privileged Caucasian and the African slave populations. These free people of color were bourgeois in wealth and cultural orientation, identifying more with the privileged white class that refused them full citizenship than with the class of fully disenfranchised African slaves. The action of Rice's novel takes place along the racial margins of nineteenth-century Louisiana, where the *gens de couleur libre* were permitted an equivocal space in which to thrive, a space already violated and invalidated. The novel illustrates the struggle of both the white and the mixed-race people to police the margins of social stratification and guard against the aspirations of the less privileged classes, such as the slaves and the free people of color who strive to rise to a level of greater freedom and respectability.

Nowhere in Anne Rice's canon of works is the issue of sexual politics more conspicuous than in *The Feast of All Saints*, where the exchange of sex for power is quite literal. The power transferred in the placage arrangement is parallel to that conferred upon women through marriage in the patriarchal system. Patriarchy is the social organization that guarantees "the overall subordination of women and dominance of men" (Connell *Masculinities* 74). Frequently, a woman's only access to power is through a marital arrangement. As in Freudian and Lacanian psychology, the woman seeks to attain the symbol of male domination and power, the phallus, through the socially sanctioned sexual alliance (Irigaray 40–41). Disenfranchised African American males have occupied a similarly subordinate position in relation to white males. The black male is forced to seek his identity and sovereignty as it is conferred by males of European descent (Connell *Masculinities* 75). Frequently, the very trappings of power and influence that the subordinated male seeks are an implicit denigration of the diversity that he embodies. The black male is compelled to struggle for the symbols of his own denigration, only allowed to be black racially if he agrees to become white culturally. In seeking identity, meaning, and prerogative from the white establishment, the person of color engages in a practice of self-denial and self-debasement. To seek the approval and enfranchisement of powerful white males, particularly through emulation, is to acknowledge their right to confer meaning and legitimacy in spite of the arbitrary nature of its historical ascendency.

In *The Feast of All Saints*, people of color, both male and female, are only permitted their truncated good fortunes through their complete subordination to the white power structure and through their repudiation of African ancestry. The principal characters adopt varying means of capitulating to the will of Caucasian males. This subordination is signified in the characters' search for paternal acceptance and favor. Marcel Ste. Marie is an adolescent male whose father, a rich, white plantation owner, is physically and emotionally distant. The father, Philippe Ferronaire, is devoted to Marcel's mother, Cecile, but his support of the children is little more than financial. He showers Marcel and his sister, Marie, with gifts during his periodic visits to New Orleans, and he retains a lawyer to look after their finances when he is absent.

Philippe's sojourns in the city do not bring any fatherly support or approval for Marcel. The father condescends to his son, whom he refers to as "spoilt" and "my little scholar," and he is disdainful toward education in general, offering his legitimate sons only enough to facilitate their management skills. Philippe allows Marcel to indulge himself. This is only because Philippe promised Marcel's mother in their original domestic arrangement that he would do so. In addition, he does not care enough about the boy to influence his actions. Indeed, Philippe's principal concern for Marcel's education is that the boy not be encouraged to harbor unrealistic expectations for his future. Marcel's lack of paternal guidance begins to manifest itself in adolescent behavioral problems, culminating in his expulsion from Monsieur de Latte's private academy. Distraught over the child's truant behavior, Cecile rashly addresses a letter of complaint to the boy's father, an act that the entire household regards as desperate and dangerous. However, they all underestimate the father's indifference toward his alternative family. Upon his next visit to New Orleans, he appears to have forgotten the entire episode and only addresses the issue after it is again brought to his attention.

Because his biological father does not perform the paternal duties of conferring social identity upon the child and ushering him into the world of meaning and respectability, Marcel seeks legitimacy and paternal acceptance elsewhere. For a time, Marcel seeks fatherly affection from an old cabinetmaker, Jean Jacques, who shares his time and his knowledge with the boy. Jean Jacques was a slave on the island of Saint Domingue during the bloody uprising against the French plantation owners. He relates to Marcel the events that led to his own liberation and, more importantly, he tells of the abduction of Cecile by the women whom Marcel had always believed were his aunts. Marcel is also fascinated with the cabinetmaker's skills, and he even envisions himself following in Jean Jacques footsteps: "If I had not been born rich, I could have learned the cabinetmaker's trade" (338). The craftsman's death is very hard for Marcel, who grieves as though he had lost his own father.

Upon the cabinetmaker's death, the boy turns to Christophe Mercier for fatherly guidance. Christophe foils Jean Jacques, representing antithetical traits in the sociocultural spectrum and hierarchy. He is a sophisticated man of learning, while Jean Jacques is a craftsman and a freed slave. As a descendent of African slaves, Jean Jacques is the repository of knowledge about a portion of Marcel's cultural heritage. Christophe is a capitulationist who initially looks only toward Europe for his cultural history.

Christophe retains an aristocratic air. He left for France at an early age and attained celebrity for his literary gifts. Upon his return, he creates a considerable stir among his young admirers in New Orleans. Christophe is a role model for youngsters like Marcel, who are awaiting their turn to travel to Europe for an education and an opportunity to live in a color-blind society. The successful gentleman intends to open a school where he will facilitate the learning and social advancement of other mixed-race people. There are rumors of his homosexuality that at first create some hesitation and suspicion toward his school. Nevertheless, Marcel and the other young men of color are desperate to enroll.

Christophe and Marcel become quite close, and it is obvious that the boy admires his teacher greatly. There is, however, no hint of any forbidden passion between the two until Marcel is openly spurned and betrayed by his father. It is at this point that the young man offers himself to his teacher, whom he suspects has always desired him. To Marcel's surprise, Christophe refuses the overture, confessing that he loves the boy but recognizes that Marcel is searching for a surrogate father. Christophe believes that the boy can never really love anyone so long as he still desperately needs fatherly affection and approval:

> It's the intensity that breaks the heart, the feeling of being lost in a world of fragmented dreams and aspirations without guidance, without some strong hand that can lead you to maturity where you will feel self-reliant at last. I don't think that you can really love anyone, Marcel, until you have that self-reliance, until the need is diminished. And I tell you right now the need in you is desperate. You laid your heart bare to that old cabinetmaker, Jean Jacques, and it was pure and unmingled with desire just as it was the first night I came home. You said to me from your soul,

"be my teacher, be my father, help me to become someone who
is valuable, someone who is good" [482].

Christophe also comments on Marcel's repressed desire for his biological
father and interprets the passion as a longing for power, which is represented by this rich white, man who strewed his "path with gold" (483).
Marcel does not love the man, but he loves the idea of the man, the representation of cultural affluence and respect.

The abandonment of Marcel by his powerful white father is emblem-
atic of the disenfranchisement and disempowerment of the *gens de couleur
libre* in the American South of the mid-nineteenth century. This group
searched for acceptance and identity from white males, but they were left
bereft of legitimacy and legal standing in a culture that refused to acknowledge them. Christophe can recognize the terrible sense of abandonment
and longing in others because he too has experienced it. He is not emotionally equipped to become a surrogate father because he also requires
reassurance from an adult male, specifically his teacher and lover, Michael,
who followed him to New Orleans to solicit his return to France.
Christophe was rescued from a menial job by the older man, educated,
and encouraged along the path to adulthood. Unlike Marcel, Christophe
actually receives the paternal support that is requisite to his maturation.
However, after achieving independence, both physically and intellectually, Christophe abandons his teacher to return to New Orleans and to
assist other young men of color. Christophe literally and figuratively kills
the father, Michael. After following Christophe to America, Michael contracts yellow fever and dies. Of course, Christophe blames himself for the
death, lamenting that the Englishman would not have been compelled to
follow had Christophe not returned to New Orleans. Christophe also
symbolically killed his father by rejecting him after assuming the mantle
of success and independence. The younger man emulates the Freudian
child who, after a brief period of homosexual identification with the father,
abandons his attraction and models his own behavior upon the father's
(Sedgewick 23).

Both of the above paternal relationships are reminiscent of the Greek
pederastic tradition in which an older man assumes responsibility for an
adolescent boy's education in culture and warfare (Greenberg 110). The
attachment is also erotic in nature because the child also learns about sex
through his experimentation with the older man. The association between
Christophe and Michael is particularly indicative of the tradition because
matches were generally only considered appropriate between members of
opposing social classes. The dominant, older man was invariably of higher

social status than his partner was, and Michael is clearly older and more affluent than Christophe is. The pederastic relation generally ended at the younger participant's advent of adulthood. In the case of Marcel and Christophe, the educational aspect of this ancient tradition is intact. However, the sexual longings remain unrealized and, for a time, unacknowledged. There is nevertheless a great deal of sexual tension between the men, particularly regarding Marcel's continued sexual liaisons with Christophe's mother, which eventually take place with the son's full knowledge and even in his own bed. It becomes obvious from the outset of the novel that Marcel pursues Juliet (the mother) because she is a replacement for Christophe. Originally, Rice had intended to make Marcel and the teacher lovers, but the publishing company preferred that Marcel remain straight, and the author conceded (Ramsland *Prism* 188).

The novel is teeming with dead or absent fathers. Cecile Ste. Marie lost her father when she was still an infant. He was a French planter who was murdered and hung on meat hooks during the slave revolts on the island of Saint Domingue. It was in this context that Marcel's aunts abducted the child, thinking at first that she was an orphan. They later refused to hand her over to her hysterical African mother. Anna Belle, the childhood friend of Marcel, witnessed her own father's murder. He was a successful freed slave who angered local whites and was slaughtered for it. The girl was then brought to New Orleans by the Old Captain, who raised her in comfort and privilege but subsequently died, leaving her to seek sponsorship elsewhere. Vincent Dazincourt, the father of Dolly Rose's dead baby, is absent from the child's life until her funeral, where he makes a conspicuous gesture of attending and paying for the services. Dolly Rose becomes hysterical and blasts Vincent publicly for refusing to support the child while she was alive. When the same man impregnates Anna Belle, he asks her to place the child with a nurse so that it will not interfere with their relationship. Later, he excuses himself from any further association with Anna Belle and their child, claiming that the placage arrangement is evil and exploitative. However, he does agree to support the mother and child financially for the remainder of their lives. Marcel and his sister, Marie, are raised almost exclusively by their mother. The father, Philippe, visits only periodically, even then offering only financial assistance. In the case of the slave Lisette, Philippe will not even acknowledge her as his daughter, let alone release her from bondage. In *The Feast of All Saints*, only one normative paternal figure is fully developed: Rudolphe Lermontant. Even he is occasionally unable to offer protective paternal care because of the limitations that discrimination and racial injustice impose.

In the placage arrangement, women become the objects of monetary exchange. Within the context of *Feast*, the settlement most frequently arises where there is no male who can assure financial solvency. This search for a match with a white male becomes a search for a sponsor. The quadroon balls are a vast marketplace, not entirely unlike the slave auction, where women of mixed race are paraded before white males who will exchange wealth and affluence for sexual favors. The negotiations for the subsequent matches involve provisions for any children—a dowry for the girls and a European education for the boys—and frequently for additional members of the extended mixed race families. Love is not a prerequisite for the union. In contemporary slang, such a sponsor would be referred to as a sugar daddy (an expression that emphasizes the paternal nature of an arrangement that is otherwise purely erotic), a prosperous male who offers a younger person economic support in exchange for intimacy over an extended period of time.

Cecile Ste. Marie has made just such an arrangement with Philippe Ferronaire long before the action of the novel begins. Although there does seem to be a good deal of real passion between Philippe and Cecile, the match is nevertheless a structured arrangement that provides the family with a house and a promise of economic security. Marie is furnished with fine clothes to increase her appeal to white males, and Marcel is provided with a first-rate education and the promise of a sojourn in Europe when he is old enough. The family has been able to live in comfort and wealth. However, they prosper only at the will of Philippe, with whom they are attentive and obsequious so as not to offend or annoy him. After Marcel makes his ill-fated journey to confront his father about broken promises, he is no longer permitted to live under Philippe's roof. The agreement between the Ste. Marie family and Philippe Ferronaire is an alternative form of slavery to a white male. The family is obliged to counterfeit the respectable, white bourgeoisie and to honor Philippe with sexual and filial devotion even though he cannot or will not acknowledge them publicly. Because the family exists only at his whim, they are not free to defy his authority.

The parallels between the Ste. Marie family and the slave population are made clear when Philippe places the slave woman ZuZu and her daughter in the Ste. Marie household. Such an act could be construed as a class distinction between the free people of color and the African slaves. However, it is also an indignity that places the Ste. Maries in the odious position of slave owners and destroys the family's illusion of legitimacy. Their household is the repository of all the master's marital infidelities. Philippe has moved the slaves from his plantation, Bontemps, to the city to hide them from his wife. In his extramarital marauding, he has raided the slave quarters. One of the objects of his lust was ZuZu, who became pregnant with his child, Lisette. Cecile is so ashamed of the kinship between her children and Lisette that she conceals the true nature of the relationship between Philippe and the slaves. She treats the slaves harshly to magnify the social distance between them. Only Lisette is willing to recognize what the members of the household have in common. When she realizes that Philippe is not going to free her as he promised, she reveals her true familial connection to Marcel and draws a parallel between the vow that Philippe has broken with her and those that he has yet to break with Marcel.

Anna Belle agrees to an arrangement between herself and Vincent Dazincourt, Philippe's brother-in-law, who is yet unmarried. The match is pushed by Anna's guardian, Madame Elsie, who has lost her own patron, the Old Captain, and now needs economic assurance for her charge. Anna is initially reluctant, even desperate to escape the inevitable union. The mercantile nature of the initial agreement is emphasized by the fact that both participants are surprised when they actually fall in love. Anna Belle objects, "I don't care anything about that man" (309). A house of her own and a promise of financial security are the compensations that Anna Belle receives for accommodating Dazincourt sexually. Vincent's own ambivalence about becoming overly committed to the relationship reveals itself in his careful efforts to avoid impregnating Anna Belle. After they do have a child, he regards it as little more than a nuisance that interferes with the relationship and forces him to close the emotional distance that he has tried to maintain. He asks Anna Belle to place the child with a nurse, an effort to deny the growing intimacy between the two lovers. One might argue that the falling out between Anna and Vincent is an illustration of the inevitable destruction that attends any of the placage matches when they are visited by real sentiment, because passion necessitates partners who are social equals. Placage, by its very nature, places a disproportionate amount of power in the hands of the male.

The social practice that treats free women of color as objects of exchange has its renegades, those who refuse to conform to the rules of propriety and discretion that have arisen around a practice that under other social conditions would be repugnant. The placage arrangement is a product of patriarchy in which those in power are able to define propriety in self-serving terms, even when such definitions contradict common social practice. Because the extramarital affairs with women of color serve the interests of the male power structure, the practice is socially coded as respectable. It is even regarded as more advantageous and legitimate than a marital union between two people of color is. However, the respectability of the institution requires that the women conform to bourgeois behavioral codes. The woman must behave like an exclusive, submissive wife even when her partner or society do not acknowledge her as such. The women of color in the novel are required to maintain exclusive relationships with their white sponsors even though there is no such commitment from the males, most of whom have a lawful marriage to a white woman. As in the cases of both Philippe and Vincent, the men are not even exclusive in their infidelities, but they require overblown gestures of bourgeois respectability from their mistresses. When Philippe observes Marcel speaking privately with Anna Belle, he forbids his son from seeing her again because she is Vincent's mistress. Similarly, Vincent is disturbed when he finds Marcel speaking privately with Anna Belle in her home, even though the couple has separated.

To optimize their appeal as marketable commodities at the quadroon balls, the women must present themselves as virgins whose chastity has been preserved exclusively for the benefit of an interested white male. The quadroon balls are a parody of the traditional debutante ball. The black women are required to behave as the traditional Southern belles do, but they are not treated with the same respect and cannot hope for a lawful union with an interested male. Dolly Rose is the foremost subversive at the gatherings. She is by no means a virgin, having had numerous affairs with white men, one of which resulted in a child. Dolly's behavior is a continual source of scandal in the community. She became hysterical at her daughter's funeral, shouting and hurling abuse at the child's father, Vincent, and consequently embarrassing all of the socially conscious *gens de couleur libre* in attendance. By the community's estimation, she returns to the quadroon balls too soon after the death of her child. Her improprieties violate the distinction between quadroon debutante and prostitute. Dolly attends the dances without attempting to maintain any facade of respectability or good intentions. Thus, the gathering is exposed as a thinly veiled exchange of sex for money. Consequently, Dolly's presence offends all those who hope to maintain the cultural distinction between proper and improper liaisons. Her household is the locale of so many brief unions with white men that it has come to be regarded as a house of prostitution. However, despite the vilification of Dolly, she turns out to be the most humane person in the community, nurturing Marie Ste. Marie back to health after the gang rape that nearly destroys her. Dolly is the only person who does not blame Marie for the violation against her.

It is one of the principal ironies of the novel that Dolly and Marie are thrown together, because heretofore they have been developed as foils:

the whore and the madonna. The empathy that these two women share collapses the social classifications that assess women of color with varying levels of respectability within the white male-power structure. The debutante and the whore, at least symbolically, become indistinguishable. This confusion of social designations becomes painfully apparent when Giselle Lermontant is accosted on the street by a white man who assumes that she is a prostitute. The Virginian has never seen a black woman dressed like a Southern belle. He thus assumes that she must be trying to make herself attractive and available to white men. The incident leads to an altercation between the Virginian and Giselle's father, Rudolphe, who is subsequently taken to court for violating interracial proprieties because he insulted a white man. The incident suggests that the very same efforts by which the free people of color try to gain respectability in the eyes of the white community frequently serve to emphasize their otherness and to undermine their attempts at social acceptance.

Marie has been even more subversive of social conventions than Dolly Rose has. The implicit objective of the placage arrangement, at least from the perspective of the free people of color, is to generate children who can pass as white. Marie is one such child who, despite her very dark mother, can easily pass for Caucasian. However, she takes the bold step of falling in love with Richard Lermontant, a man of color. From the perspective of Marie's mother and aunts, a match with Richard would be atavistic, turning backward the program of racial synthesis and reinfusing the family line with African blood. However, Marie is adamant that she will not be "forced into the arms of a man she could not marry" (200). It is this naive virtue that paradoxically destroys and preserves her. After Philippe dies unexpectedly without leaving provisions for the family, Cecile insists that Marie establish an alliance with a rich, white gentleman who can provide for the Ste. Marie family, including the disenfranchised, disillusioned Marcel. In her desperate effort to escape her mother's plans for her, Marie turns to the vindictive Lisette, who feigns concern and promises to work a charm that will make white men lose interest in the young girl. The vow turns out to be an equivocation. White men do indeed lose interest in her. However, this is not because of Lola DeDe's voodoo, but because Marie is the victim of an orchestrated gang rape by a group of white men at DeDe's establishment.

The result of Marie's victimization is paradoxical. In the eyes of her mother, she is "ruined," and the implications of this term are not lost on the young girl. Cecile sees her daughter only as a financial asset that has been rendered valueless. Her exchange value among white men was determined in large part by her virginity, which has been dramatically, even publicly lost. Both mother and daughter have internalized the whore/ madonna complex. Cecile can recognize no middle ground between purity and absolute depravity. She considers Marie responsible for the rape, and Marie silently concurs, assuming that she has no options in life but to become a prostitute. Marie takes up residence with Dolly Rose. However, consistent with the poem that is the preface to the novel, Donne's "Holy Sonnet: Batter My Heart," Marie's happiness is actually facilitated by her victimization. Donne concludes his sonnet:

> Take me to you, imprison me, for I,
> Except you enthrall me, shall never be free,
> Nor ever chaste, except you ravish me.

Like the speaker of the poem, Marie's dream of freedom and purity is only accomplished by suffering. Considered spoiled merchandise by the community, Marie is left alone to marry Richard.

The union between Marie Ste. Marie and Richard Lermontant is perhaps the most culturally subversive moment within the novel. It undermines the principles of two very distinct segments of the *gens de couleur libre* community: the black bourgeoisie and the black aristocracy. The bourgeoisie, represented by the Lermontants, must compromise their highly evolved, rigorous concepts of decency and their hyperconsciousness of morality and decorum. Whereas the family was sympathetic toward Marie following her rape, they could not abide her residence with Dolly Rose, an arrangement that simply antagonized an already delicate situation. The Ste. Maries sacrifice both their hope for a life of continued privilege and leisure and their program for breeding white progeny. The Ste. Maries regard the Lermontants as a respectable, but socially inferior, family from the laboring class. The two factors that unify these groups are their abiding concern for the advancement and maintenance of the family, community, and race and their thinly veiled self-loathing. Both groups are chasing after that phantom whiteness. However, each group has a different view of what it means to be white. The Lermontants assess whiteness as self-respect, middle-class values, and financial independence, while the Ste. Maries perceive whiteness in terms of skin tone, wealth, and leisure.

The desire to escape the stigma of blackness is the unifying feature of the *gens de couleur libre*. Most of the characters are searching for the approval of the "great white father" in one of his forms: corporeal, economic, or social. The examples of racial self-loathing abound within the novel. In contemporary American culture, the racial divide between white and black is strictly policed. The concept of hypodecent, which holds that one drop of African blood makes an individual completely black, governs our racial ideology (Kinlaw and Kasee 224). The people of color in *Feast* recognize varying degrees of ethnicity, which are in turn related to the gradations of social class. Those who occupy the position closest to physical whiteness are the most admired within the community. Marie Ste. Marie is considered very attractive because she is a woman of color who can pass for white. The desire to be white within the community is so strong that it can even breed contempt within a mother for her own daughter. Cecile is openly hostile and contemptuous toward Marie. After the death of Philippe, Cecile finally admits that she has been jealous of Marie's light skin since the girl was born. Cecile's loathing of her own blackness reveals itself in her treatment of the house slaves, ZuZu and Lisette. The presence of the mother and daughter in the house is a constant reminder of Cecile's own African heritage, of her affinity with people in bondage. She is particularly scandalized by Lisette, whose presence reminds her of her children's own precarious social position. Only random chance has created her family's freedom and prosperity. Lisette reminds Cecile that the Ste. Maries are not racially superior to "American Negroes" (Richard Lermontant's expression).

The Lermontants and the rest of the black bourgeoisie also exhibit signs of self-loathing despite their ostensible community pride. Because they remind him of racial oppression, Richard is afraid of "all things African" (159), and he is convinced of his own social superiority to anyone who is obviously more African than he is. While he maintains a scrupulous politeness toward Anna Belle, he nevertheless admits that he could never marry such a woman because her facial features, a "broad nose" and a "full mouth" (159), are so distinctly African. Such a marriage would undermine the family's project of interracial synthesis. Richard's interest in Marie may be traced to the same impulse because she can easily pass for a Caucasian and would serve to lighten the family bloodline. Richard's brothers, who moved to France where they were legally permitted to marry white women, have exhibited the same preoccupation with racial obfuscation. The family has taken great care to marry Giselle properly, arranging an attachment to a respectable family in Charleston.

Rudolphe, the Lermontant patriarch, reveals his own prejudice toward his African heritage through his appropriation of white, middle-class values and behavioral codes. His effort to emulate white culture is a repudiation of half his heritage. He has so fully internalized his own affinity with middle-class culture that his failure to achieve complete social parity torments him. He resents his inability to vote, and the incident involving the molestation of his daughter and his own subsequent arrest forced him to focus on the legal handicaps that he and his community suffer. At the trial, he defends himself by demonstrating that he is not a threat to the white community, but is culturally indistinguishable from it. He brings his white neighbors to testify to his integrity and his complete conformity to the social values that the white community has created. He is acquitted because he was behaving in a way consistent with traditional values of honor and family stability, established over a period of many generations. Of course, examples of discrimination and social injustice would and should infuriate anyone. However, Rudolphe does not despise discrimination against people of African dissent in general. His principles are a form of capitulationism. He believes he should be treated well because he has achieved bourgeois respectability.

Rudolphe is preoccupied with white notions of decency and decorum, particularly when it comes to sexuality and gender. He despises Dolly Rose for her disregard of the conventions of courtship and for living a disreputable life. He is even willing to renounce Marie for unwisely allying herself with the fallen woman after Marie's savage rape. Whereas he had previously regarded her as an appropriate bride for his son, Rudolphe quickly forbids Richard even to visit her at Dolly's residence. Furthermore, there is an element of implicit blame in his attitude toward Marie. Despite his ostensible sympathy for the young woman, he clearly holds her partially responsible for her own victimization; in his view, she should never have gone to Lola DeDe's. To his credit, he does finally allow his son to rescue and marry Marie, but he does so only after the problem of social stigma has been resolved. There is an obvious disdain within the Lermontant household for those women, such as Cecile, who ally themselves with white men. This is not because the alliance is interracial, but because it is not entirely respectable, as the two partners cannot by law marry. Rudolphe initially warns his son against becoming involved with Marie because, in his words, "girls like that always follow in their mother's footsteps" (136). The Lermontants also clearly share white, middle-class society's abhorrence for homosexuality. Rudolphe magnanimously agrees to allow his son to attend Christophe's new school despite rumors of the teacher's sexual appetites and over the objections and scandal of Richard's older brother. After Marcel has been cast out of his father's house, Rudolphe objects to the boy's residence with Christophe, prompting the teacher's outburst: "If you still don't trust me with the tender youth of this community, why don't you just shut down my school?" (472).

The black bourgeoisie reveal their contempt for their African ancestry by their silent acquiescence to the institution of slavery. Many of the prosperous families own slaves themselves, and they refuse to acknowledge their affinity to the oppressed. The author remarks that the Lermontants were unwilling to see the racial hypocrisy and fragility of their lives by refusing to acknowledge their own blackness: "Their own world was magnificently constructed for forgetting that, the Lermontant's household itself a veritable citadel, but all of them were fortified in a thousand ways" (357). The most memorable episode exhibiting the willful blindness of the *gens de couleur libre* involves Christophe's effort to educate his slave, Bubbles. When the teacher permits the servant to sit at the back of the room during class, the entire student body, Marcel excepted, withdraws from school; some do so on that very day. Faced with the failure of his formerly successful academy, Christophe visits Rudolphe Lermontant, who explains the families' resistance. The people of color must maintain a clear distinction between themselves and the slave population to convince whites that they are better than slaves and, therefore, deserve to be treated differently:

> "We're talking about a caste, Christophe, that has won its precarious place in this corrupt quagmire by asserting over and over that it is composed of men who are better than and different from slaves! We get respect in one way, Christophe, and that is by insisting ourselves on what we are. Men of property, men of breeding, men of education, and men of family. But if we drink with slaves, marry slaves, sit down in our parlors with slaves or in our dining rooms or in our classrooms, then men will treat us as if we were no better" [279].

Despite his hypocrisy, Rudolphe still makes room for compassion. He tells Christophe that if he educates the slave in private, the community will admire him for his philanthropy. Rudolphe's objections reveal the inherently precarious nature of racial classifications within the novel. The harder that the *gens de couleur libre* try to maintain a social and racial distinction between themselves and slaves, the more clearly they concede that the difference is only nominal and that their own good fortune is only happenstance. The destabilizing of racial divisions extends to include the white population. The mixed-race characters within the novel have implicitly recognized the permeable line between "black" and "colored," but they have continued to regard white as an inviolable ideal of racial purity and social privilege. They do not see that racial ideology also victimizes the white characters—of course, not to the same extent as the black characters. Not unlike Lacan's phallic symbol of power, meaning, and privilege (Sarup 123), whiteness is not a condition that anyone actually possesses. It is an ideal that initiates racial meaning, an ideal against which ethnicity is defined and evaluated. Everyone (even whites) falls short of this ideal and is symbolically castrated or disempowered.

The social system that permits Philippe Ferronaire to prosper and to domineer over people of mixed race also sets limits on his own freedoms. The rules of racial engagement keep Philippe in a loveless marriage to Aglae, whom he refers to as a "reptile in the guise of a woman" (452). The marriage is devoid of passion, and Philippe is increasingly aware that his wife does not respect him; she criticizes and belittles him with her silence. He is concerned that people will learn that he has no ambition to wield the power thrust upon him, the burden of running a plantation. His life on the farm is so demoralizing that only his visits to the city can assuage his declining self-image. He feels white—privileged, respected, and powerful—only in relation to his black family, the Ste. Maries, where he is treated with deference, like a visiting dignitary (324–27). "White" has meaning only in relation to "not white." In the context of "all white," the social distinction is indistinct, losing all of its defining attributes and exposing the racial fiction.

Philippe is bridled by the same social conventions that award him prerogative. He cannot marry the woman he really loves, Cecile, and he cannot fulfill his promises to the family that pays him the respect that he thinks he deserves. His failure to manage the plantation forces him to renege on his vow to send Marcel to France and to arrange a hasty marriage between Marie and Richard, a match about which he had previously expressed reservations. The power and privilege that had previously been representative of his right to domineer over the Ste. Marie household becomes a burden and a bondage. The mismanagement of the plantation, which results in its seizure by his wife and his brother-in-law, is in all probability the price of his maintaining two households in luxury. Thus, the signs of his social affluence are what eventually deprive him of his power. After his ouster, he takes up residence in the Ste. Marie household, signifying his own enfeeblement and the collapsing of the socioracial divisions. Ironically, once he is finally in a position to make a lasting emotional commitment to the Ste. Marie family, he is no longer socially or financially capable of it; he cannot fulfill his portion of the original domestic arrangement.

The predicament of Vincent Dazincourt is not unlike Philippe's. It becomes clear that Vincent's relationship with Anna Belle is the most vital and passionate of his life, and yet he is not allowed the sanction of marriage and is eventually forced to abandon the union. Moreover, he abhors the brutality of slavery, but as a white plantation owner, he is forced by economic necessity to participate in the institution nonetheless. His frequent altruistic gestures toward the people of color are distinctly patronizing, exposing a fundamental belief in his own superiority, a belief that constantly dictates his behavior. The assumption that he must look after these people requires that he place himself in a number of unpleasant, even dangerous situations. In the dynamics of power, the submissive partner controls the dominating partner insofar as the submissive's own behavior frequently dictates when and how the dominant must act. Control requires resistance, and resistance dictates and necessitates the action of the controller (Chancer 50). Vincent is constantly cleaning up messes. He shoulders the financial burden of the funeral for Dolly Rose's child. He rescues Christophe from a white planter, angry because the teacher has had an affair with Dolly Rose. He places himself in mortal danger by challenging and killing the rapists of Marie. As a white man, Vincent does not possess power so much as a series of odious obligations, a burden that he might wish to pass. At the conclusion of the novel, he longs for his child to live in a place where the races reside in peace, and he chooses not to participate in the placage institution any longer, believing that it unsettles and blurs racial boundaries. The conflicts of race, gender, and class have kept Vincent Dazincourt engaged, bound by social convention, unable to extricate himself from entanglements that are his social duty to resolve. The obligations of the white patriarch, in essence, victimize the victimizer.

The power associated with whiteness certainly does not reside with the Caucasian women in the novel. Philippe's wife, Aglae, has little control over her life, although she is able to assume more by the conclusion of the narrative. She is obliged to marry a man whom she does not love or even respect to fulfill an economic arrangement between her father and her husband. The financial predicament of the men who surround her dictate the conditions of her life. Her father seeks a spouse for her, requiring that the husband manage the plantation since her brother, Vincent, is not yet old enough to assume the responsibility. Little or no thought is given to Aglae's own happiness, nor is there any evaluation of her own ability to operate a plantation, a task that eventually falls upon her regardless of her father's precautionary actions. Her life includes many of the same symbols of submission and servitude as those in the lives of the free people of color. Although she frequently disapproves of her husband's actions, she is essentially powerless to deter him. Knowing that he keeps a separate household and family in the city, she cannot even speak against the practice since modesty and social convention dictate that she feign ignorance. Moreover, her husband treats her with contempt and tries to embarrass her publicly because he senses her disapproval. He furnishes the house of his mistress with items taken from the plantation, some of which belong to his wife, a sign that he has equal disregard for all of the women in his life. This circulation of objects of value among those women with whom he is sexually engaged further collapses the social distinction between wife, mistress, and slave, implicating all the women in the economy of sex and money.

Any priority that Aglae occupies in Philippe's obligations is dictated entirely by racial ideology and economic necessity. Her legitimate marriage to Philippe exists because he needs her money and because the law will not sanction a match between a white male and a woman of African descent. However, it is this very legitimacy that provides Aglae with the principal advantage she possesses over the mistresses. She has legal standing within the community as a spouse and as a white woman. When she discovers the mismanagement of the plantation, she has the legal standing to wrestle it away from Philippe's poor husbandry, whereas Cecile must fend for herself financially after the ruin of the Ferronaire fortunes. However, one of the great ironies of the racial separation of the two households is that Philippe, his wife, and their sons have had to labor to keep the Ste. Marie household in aristocratic idleness. Philippe's legitimate sons do not get the extravagant education that Marcel receives. The true symbol of Philippe's affluence is not the magnificence of Bontemps nor the number of his slaves, but his ability to maintain a mistress in wealth and leisure. Thus, Aglae possesses few of the advantages that are attached to whiteness and all of the handicaps that are attached to womanhood in a patriarchal system.

The analysis of racial divisions within the novel is engaged at the broad level of thematics and in the details of characterization and incident. Nowhere is the fraudulent nature of racial divisions more obvious than in the imagery of skin tone. Physical anthropologists classify race by facial features because skin tones vary greatly within a single racial classification. There is frequently little or no difference between the skin tone of Asians, such as the Chinese, and Caucasians, such as the northern Europeans. Moreover, there is not a difference between the complexion of many Caucasians from the Asian subcontinent, specifically India, and the darkest Africans. Despite the fluidity of skin tones among races, the concept of race in America is reduced to the dichotomous hues of black and white. However, this racial binary of white and black is deconstructed because it does not refer to actual ethnic categories or to physical characteristics, but only to class and social convention.

Skin tone as an indicator of race or ethnicity is destabilized at the very outset of the novel. Cecile is described as a "white woman carved in black stone" (321), Caucasian features with dark skin. Thus, she could be justifiably labeled as Caucasian or white. Moreover, her lifestyle is one of leisure and wealth, privilege that exceeds that of other blacks. Yet she is nonetheless subject to many significant social handicaps as a consequence of racial presumptions. Marie is the most problematic figure because she is socially a black woman who is completely white in feature, flesh tone, and lifestyle. Only her history and ancestry make her black. Even the issue of legal legitimacy is nullified because if she could escape her past and her family, she could pass as white and enjoy all the privileges and recognitions that are inherent in that social category. Marcel recognizes that the boundaries of race are unstable. He observes that there are many slaves who actually have lighter skin than he does. The ideology of white and black is a social construct that is situated geographically and historically; it refers to perceptions of legitimacy and value that are based on variations in flesh tone rather than on scientific observation. Thus, white or black does not refer to race; it refers to law, history, culture, and convention.

Within the novel, the idea of whiteness as a racial category is contextually and geographically situated. The authority of whiteness resides in the presumption that it is a fundamental biological category that is natural, transcultural, and transhistorical. However, Rice has labored to demonstrate that America's pseudoscientific racial ideology does not even extend into those countries that are traditionally considered white by Americans. It is a cultural tradition of the *gens de couleur libre* to send their young males to France when they have reached adolescence so that they can mature in an environment that considers them men, one that will regard them as the social equals of Caucasians. Several brief episodes in the novel illustrate the desperation with which the characters seek to escape to the more permissive environment. Charles Roget returns from France for only one day to settle issues surrounding his inheritance. This is in spite of the devastating impact that the news has on his family. He proclaims that "he would not spend one night on southern soil" and that he has a white fiancée in France who could not accompany him because he feared physical injury or prosecution (171). In another incident, a celebrated young sculptor, Narcisse Cruzat, famous for his "funereal art" displayed throughout the city, leaves to study Italian sculpture in Europe, acknowledging that in America he will never be fully appreciated (383–85). The disdain that Christophe's English lover, Michael, expresses also illustrates that American racial philosophy does not necessarily cross national borders. He has followed Christophe to New Orleans to convince him to return to Europe to escape the degradations of racism.

The desire to escape from a culture that does not recognize subtle variations in racial heritage is perhaps the defining attribute of Rice's free people of color. Marcel's Aunt Josette reveals the family plan to engender white children by continuing the process of marrying Caucasian men. Marcel himself has been unwilling to recognize his own African heritage or his own marginality. Thus, his ill-fated trip to Philippe's plantation that resulted in a violent repudiation by his father. Marcel's coming of age necessitates that he accept his African ancestry, first by learning of the historical heritage and then by recognizing and embracing his own marginality. Rice has defined Marcel's struggle as the discovery that he is black (Riley 129). His decision to become a daguerreotypist to make a career of photographing his people represents his acceptance of his ethnicity, his history, and his community. It also represents the cessation of his identification with, and emulation of, white culture. He is preserving the fragile culture of the *gens de couleur libre* in photographic images, thus embracing rather than escaping his African cultural heritage. The same process occurs with many other characters. Christophe returns to New Orleans from his privileged, celebrated life in France to stop running from his ancestry and to make a contribution to his community. Moreover, Anna Belle says that she is not going to raise her child to loath his African heritage or to long for his escape to France. By silently acquiescing to American racism through class insolence, self-loathing, or escape, the free people of color are facilitating and legitimizing a repugnant institution, one that will never be changed until there is unity and self-respect within the community.

The above embrace of blackness, however, is one of the ways in which the politics of the novel are compromised. After herculean efforts to dismantle the overly simplistic, dichotomous notions of race within American culture, the author reinstates that very same ideology. The author does not suggest that black is inferior, of course, but she suggests that blackness exists as a distinct racial classification. The truly revolutionary idea of the novel is inherent in the dissolution of racial categories. Once the opposition of white and black is reinstalled, the accompanying devaluing of the latter category will follow. Whereas the recognition and acceptance of African heritage constitutes an advancement, the capitulation to the simplistic racial binary is not. Marcel must find that he is both black and white, a deserving and fully enfranchised inheritor of both cultural legacies. To be truly free and equal, Marcel must be allowed his whiteness and his blackness, so long as the former category does not necessitate the degradation and exploitation of the latter. The longing for the "great white father" was not a productive pursuit for the characters of the novel because it gave the white establishment all of the powers for conferring legitimacy. However, to define oneself in opposition to a standard is to legitimize that standard by expressing a faith in its temporal priority and by implicitly accepting the principles upon which the opposition is constructed.

As in many of her novels, in *The Feast of All Saints*, Rice reveals an unquestioning confidence in the legitimacy of middle class values, almost as though the category were empty of any sociopolitical content, a part of natural law. This assumption is central to American cultural ideology, and it accounts for much social and political discrimination. Those who do not accept middle-class values are marginalized socially, and they are frequently denigrated in political discourse. The middle-class ideal of honest, hard work is held up as a panacea for the conflicts of the novel. The idle aristocrats need to be knocked off their thrones and earn a living in a traditional fashion rather than being kept and provided for by rich whites. Marcel is finally put to work as a completely self-reliant photographer. Christophe abandons his comfortable life in Europe under the sponsorship of Michael to open an academy for the privileged children of the *gens de couleur libre*. Marie is rescued from a life of shame by residing in Dolly Rose's residence, where she is remarkably comfortable, and she is swept off to a life as a respectable wife to Richard Lermontant. The family even devises a plan for salvaging Marie's reputation so that she can live up to the standards of decorum and decency that are expected of a middle-class housewife and so that scandal will not sully Lermontant's public image. The implication of the episode is that if there had not been a means of salvaging Marie's reputation by sending the couple to France, the Lermontants would have had a compelling reason not to accept her into the family. The narrative suggests that Marie is well situated in a family that is so moralistic and preoccupied by public image that they are afraid to be kind to a victim of gang rape. Of course, the excuse for their behavior is predictably economic. The patriarch of the family resists because scandal would harm his business interests and the good name that they have created over several generations.

The narrative implies that people of African ancestry can achieve increased social acceptance and affluence if they are willing to emulate white, middle-class values. Rice does little to interrogate the politics of that expectation. Clearly the reason for the Lermontants' success and public respect is because the community deems them safe. They have the same values, goals, and concerns as the white populace. Thus, they can be expected to behave in a predictable, socially constructive fashion. They will not challenge the established power imbalance. When Rudolphe is prosecuted, he is only able to escape punishment because he is perceived as having acted in accordance with values that the middle class deem sacred: the protection of family and home. He even rallies the support of white neighbors who can testify to his inoffensiveness, an observation that is composed of a repudiation of his African heritage, which is considered threatening to the white establishment.

To assume the values of the American middle class is to endorse and even facilitate various forms of subordination. Through acceptance of class ideology, the Lermontants technically support the indefensible institution of slavery. Even had they not been slave owners themselves, they would have been guilty of perpetuating the infamy. By enthusiastically policing the boundaries between themselves and the slave population, they suggest that the slaves deserve bondage while the Lermontants deserve privilege and respect. The entire project of the novel is based on the author's fascination with the *gens de couleur libre*'s desire and ability to emulate European culture despite adversity. Rice became interested in these people when she learned that they had published one of the first literary journals in America. Thus, her interest in them stems from those unexpected features of their lives, specifically ones borrowed from the European traditions.

The slave and African populations are dehumanized and trivialized within the narrative. They are, with few exceptions, either caricatures or villains. Only one slave, Lisette, is fully developed, and she is portrayed as hateful, vindictive, and vicious. She virtually destroys the most innocent character in the novel in a means that is distinctly African, taking Marie to a voodoo priestess. Many of the slaves' names are distinctly African (e.g., DeDe and ZuZu), suggesting their cultural marginality, while the names of the black bourgeoisie are French, a language traditionally associated with sophisticated European culture. Some slaves even have clown names, such as Bubbles, who despite his faithfulness and hard work is nonetheless portrayed as only partially human. The author even compares his appearance to that of a monkey, and while her intentions are clearly to rehabilitate this traditional racist simile, making it a compliment rather than an offense, she is unsuccessful. Philippe's driver is the epitome of loyalty and good sense, rescuing Marcel from his father's wrath after the boy unwisely breaches the divide between his father's two discrete worlds. However, the slave is not developed as a personality, remaining only a faceless messenger and deliveryman whom service and a lifetime of submission has degraded.

The middle-class traditions advocated in the novel are constructed

upon gender subordination as well. Women are domesticated and com-
modified, expected to maintain their virginity to guarantee their value in
the marriage marketplace. I have already discussed the "ruining" of Marie
as a marriageable object by rape. The women in the novel are used to
advance the class and economic status of the other characters, frequently
the men. Marie is urged to attend the quadroon balls for her brother, who
has recently been disinherited and has little other chance of advancement.
Anna Belle is urged into the arms of Vincent to fill the financial gap created by the death of the Old Captain, her white benefactor. Dolly Rose's
desperate promiscuity interrogates the economic and exploitative nature
of the placage arrangement. The novel attempts to rehabilitate and
redefine the morality of these frequently adulterous, loveless, and demean-
ing relationships by making them an exclusive commitment of the woman,
while the man is free to roam, spreading his seed throughout the land.
The fidelity of the woman is required to maintain a quasi-respectability
for the mistress and the family. However, the presence of Dolly Rose
reveals the goal of the financial arrangement at the heart of these pre-
tenses to be middle-class respectability, an arrangement that in many ways
resembles her prostitution. Moreover, the women are frequently left alone
to raise the subsequent family after the white males grow tired of them.
The novel includes several abandoned women, particularly Juliet,
Christophe's mother, whose white lovers eventually lost interest in her.
The abandonment has taken a toll on her psychologically; most people
think that she is mad. Even Cecile was the lover of Philippe's father-in-
law before she became involved with Philippe himself.

Vincent, who is a representation of misguided compassion and un-
knowing complicity in exploitation, leaves Anna Belle, citing the immoral-
ity of the adulterous relations between them. While he is sympathetic and
provides for the family, he is nevertheless leaving a new mother to raise
a child by herself. Moreover, if Vincent's repudiation of the institution of
interracial matches between freed women and white planters is intended
to be the author's judgment on the subject (and it seems to be), then there
is much to be criticized within the novel. Vincent concludes that the
whole community of mixed-race people never should have existed. They
are the product of "carelessness and carnality" (588). He offers these opin-
ions in the context of concern for the woman he is preparing to abandon.
Moreover, his eugenic perspective would invalidate and wipe away a community of people who are generally happy and prosperous, simply because
they do not fit into neat racial and social categories. He would wipe away
people who are far more cultured, sophisticated, and talented than he is.
He blames a racist culture for his perspective. He makes no effort to defy

convention by embracing the woman he loves and their child, a position that would be truly revolutionary. Instead, he surrenders to established notions of social propriety, the same that have vexed the characters throughout the novel. Finally, in the context of the patriarchal system and a narrative that is devoted to characters who search unsuccessfully for legitimacy from the white-male establishment, allowing the final word to be pronounced by a white patriarch who has been implicated in the system all along is particularly insidious. Vincent refuses to confer legitimacy and meaning on the relationship, the child, or the community that he has helped to create. The conclusion that Marcel reaches regarding the appropriate focus of his admiration and expectations is worthy of inquiry as well. The author implies that the boy needs to accept his African heritage and to abandon his efforts to gain validation from white culture. This determination could be well taken if it meant that he accepted and appreciated his African ancestry. However, it restores the racial dichotomy that the novel has taken such pains to dismantle. It also seems to advocate the tradition of hypodescent, in which a single drop of African blood makes the individual totally black. Marcel is as Caucasian as he is African, both physically and culturally. Moreover, the traditional racial categories have been rendered virtually meaningless through the collapsing of cultural and racial markers within *Feast*. However, at the conclusion, the author points back to those same signs of difference as if they were completely intact and stable. Marcel's lot is to be torn between two worlds, each of which he has a considerable investment in, and it is no more appropriate for him to identify completely with African culture than it was for him to focus exclusively on Caucasian culture.

Rice's diagnosis for complete freedom and self-respect among the *gens de couleur libre* involves the most trite conclusion of the identity-politics movement: accept who you are. Whereas there is much wisdom and truth in this assertion, as the resolution of an otherwise deconstructed debate about race, class, and gender, the customary argument about embracing one's heritage seems overly simplistic, particularly since the novel so effectively erases the boundaries between traditional categories upon which the conclusion relies. The novel even comes close to condemning interracial matches simply because the issue of those relations will not be completely white. Thus, again it advocates a resegregation and simplification of racial and ethnic classifications. Perhaps the novelist has chosen this conventional resolution as a commercial consideration, because it is hard to imagine a completely deconstructed conclusion appealing to a very wide audience. Of course, the novel did not achieve the success that Rice was expecting, regardless of this attention to audience.

Chapter 3

THE PURLOINED PENIS:
CASTRATION ANXIETY
IN *CRY TO HEAVEN*

When Anne Rice began to research her third novel, she hoped to write the story of a virtuoso violinist living in France during the revolution. However, in the course of her study, she came upon a description of the castrated singers of the Italian opera and became fascinated with their suffering. With the castrati, she encountered a group of men who were simultaneously regarded as monsters and as cultural icons, a contrast that created fruitful ground for the examination of various moral and ethical conflicts. For Rice, these singers came to signify androgyny and "unrestrained sexual energy" (Ramsland *Prism* 197), and they continued the author's focus upon the struggles of socially marginalized groups.

The novel focuses on Tonio, a fourteen-year-old boy who is forcibly castrated by his father and driven out of his native Venice, where he had stood to inherit the family legacy in his father's place. The castration also severed the close relationship that the boy had always enjoyed with his mother. Whether Rice composed this story and then recognized its Freudian implications or whether she specifically devised the plot to conform to the oedipal triangle is immaterial. The parallels between the plot and Freud's family romance are unmistakable. Indeed, the events of the novel often amount to a literalization of psychoanalytic theories, specifically those developed by Jacques Lacan in his resurrection and revision of Freud's seminal research. Before Lacan, the psychoanalytic approach to literature was to examine the work as a symptom of the author's own pathologies; the text was the outpouring of the writer's repressed impulses and desires. Lacan's approach, which he made famous in his celebrated "Seminar on *The Purloined Letter*," was to examine the text as independent of its author's potential neuroses (Felman 133). Although I believe that a study of Anne Rice's various fixations would be quite compelling, such an approach lies outside the scope of this discussion.

Freud maintained that the child, at an early age, develops an amorous fixation upon the mother, desiring to be the sole focus of her affections. At the same time, the child begins to resent the father, the rival for the mother's love. This sentiment even leads to fantasies of killing the father and possessing the mother. The child eventually abandons his incestuous longings because he fears castration at the father's hands. The father's disruption of the child's desires becomes the paradigm for all the power that the child will encounter in life: "The Oedipal Complex is the beginning of morality, conscience, law, and all forms of authority" (Sarup 4–5). Obstructed in his desire for the mother, the child turns toward identification with the father, hoping through emulation to possess a woman who is a replacement for the lost mother.

The construction of the female child's sexual identity runs parallel to the male's until the girl realizes that she does not possess a penis, the father's identifying characteristic and the symbol of his dominance. The child begins to resent the mother, whom she blames for depriving her of the privileged sexual organ. She longs to possess her father and, through him, to obtain a penis. This is the beginning of sexual desire. This longing is eventually replaced by the wish to have a fetus in her womb (Irigaray 40–41). Feminist theorists have accused Freud of being a phallocrat because he portrays the female's condition as one of absence, thus inherently inferior to the male's. The woman is defined sexually by a "lack" or an emptiness (Irigaray 23). Freud suggests that through her erotic desire to possess a man, the woman actually longs to obtain the power and authority associated with the phallus.

Rice was certainly familiar with these theories. In her biography, she comments on the oedipal longings of her vampires (Ramsland *Prism* 253). The human Lestat is despised by his father and his brothers, but he is dearly loved by his mother, with whom he shares a close relationship. After the young man's transformation, he learns of his mother's impending death and rescues her by sharing his "dark gift," hoping that they will be joined eternally. Eventually, he becomes the guardian of his blinded father, whose approval Lestat continues to seek even after he becomes a vampire. All of the elements of the family drama are present in this particular portrayal, but here the young man's conflict is not resolved in the usual fashion. Indeed, the situation concludes with the fulfillment of the oedipal fantasy. The young man is able to supplant and gain control over the father and to possess the mother permanently. The threat of castration is removed once Lestat is no longer human and is no longer a sexual being in any traditional sense.

The contemporary revision of Freudian theory that psychoanalyst Jacques Lacan developed is a more appropriate model for the analysis of Rice's *Cry to Heaven*. Lacan's reading of Freud has become popular among literary critics because it involves a revision of the now-mythic ideas along post-structuralist lines, examining their relationship to language. Lacan's most innovative idea was his postulation of the mirror stage of human development, a stage fundamental to the formation of subjectivity. Before the age of 18 months, the child has no sense of physical unity, perceiving itself as a fragmentary collection of bodily functions associated with eating, defecating, and so on (Lee 25). During the mirror stage, the child is first confronted with an image of itself as a unified whole, and the child perceives the mother's presence as part of this totality. Thus, the infant develops a very close bond with the mother, perceiving her to be an extension of the self. This image of wholeness that the child develops during the mirror stage will be one of the most self-alienating events in its psychic development because it will never be able to recreate the sense of unity and completion that it experiences in its mother's arms (Ragland-Sullivan 275). Eventually, the father intercedes, breaking the mother-infant dyad with the prohibition "no," which is a representation of authority and the incest taboo. This is termed the Name-of-the-Father, and it is the beginning of law and social consciousness within the child—what Freud would have called the superego. The mirror-stage union of mother and child is Lacan's revision of the Freudian oedipal desire, and the separation of the child from his mother by the law of the father is Lacan's castration complex (Ragland-Sullivan 55). The child permanently loses its sense of completeness; his life will be spent in a futile effort to regain that lost unity (*jouissance*) through its objects of desire (Ragland-Sullivan 75).

Chief among the signifiers within the Lacanian oedipal conflict is the phallus, the symbol of sexual difference and the representation both of the father's power and of his possession of the mother. The phallus, the father's distinguishing characteristic, intervenes within the mother-infant dyad, breaking the union and implanting the idea of sexual difference in the child's consciousness. The research of the French linguist Ferdinand de Saussure is vital to understanding Lacan's theory of the phallus. For Saussure, meaning in language is indefinitely deferred because it is produced by the distinction between terms that stand in opposition to each other—male/female, good/evil, masculine/feminine, etcetera—and because signifiers (words) do not create any universal mental images in the minds of all listeners or readers. Lacan accepted and applied Saussure's theories. However, he identified signifiers that he termed "points de capton," which transcend difference and rivet the signifying chain by maintaining a stable signification. Chief among these is the phallus, which provides the stable ground upon which the endless deflections of the signifying chain rest (Lee 61). "The Phallic signifier is the first pure signifier of difference ... it is, therefore, the reference point for an infant's development of the capacity to use symbols as signifiers" (Ragland-Sullivan 281). The first binary opposition, and the one that begins the child's socialization and language acquisition, refers to sexual difference. The phallus thus initiates the subject's encounter with language. Feminist intellectuals have attacked this theory as phallocentric because it identifies the male organ as the privileged signifier. Such objections are understandable. However, Lacan differentiated between the phallus and the penis, maintaining that no one, male or female, actually possesses the phallus. It is the idealization of the father's power; it is the representation of the symbolic father (Silverman 101). The male child does not possess the phallus any more than the female does, and the extent to which both sexes fall short of this ideal determines secondary castration.

According to Lacanian psychoanalytic theory, the child is castrated yet a second time by learning a language that will forever perpetuate his sense of fragmentation. In opposition to Freud and subsequent ego-psychology, Lacan argued against the notion that an individual possesses a unified and conscious ego, a stable sense of self that is at the center of being. He replaces the ego with the subject, a construct of language and a concept more closely allied to Freud's id than to his ego (Gallop 96–102). The subject is composed of the unstable and ever-shifting significations of language. The child arrives at a sense of self by being exposed to the preexisting language categories that refer only imperfectly to the idea of self. In other words, the individual does not produce language, but language produces the individual. This lack of control is parallel to the child's need to capitulate to the father's injunction against the oedipal union, and thus it is another castration. The recognition of this castrated state leads to a desire for lost wholeness, and this desire leads to the need to articulate the subject's emptiness and fragmentation, so the child is thrust into language (Ragland-Sullivan 271).

Lacan's foray into literary criticism began with his "Seminar on *The Purloined Letter*," in which he argued that the stolen missive of Poe's short story, the letter whose content is never revealed, is representative of the emptiness of the signifier. Lacan identifies three triangles in which the characters' subjectivity is determined by their varying, shifting relationships to the stolen letter. In these formations, one person conceals the letter by leaving it in plain view, another does not see the letter at all, and the third recognizes the first's deception and pilfers the note. Lacan argues that the subjectivity of the participants in these parallel situations are constituted by the character's relation to the letter (signifier), to the symbolic order of language. Lacan thus maintains that human subjectivity is created by language (Gallop 64–73). Lacan's insights into Poe's short story are useful in the analysis of Anne Rice's third novel, in which similar relational triangles are constructed. For Rice, it is the phallus that determines identity and initiates signification.

Lacan also offers an interpretation of Shakespeare's *Hamlet*, arguing that the play is concerned with "desire and mourning" (Lee 109). Rice's *Cry to Heaven* addresses similar themes. There are multiple parallels between the novel and the play: the loss of a father, an incestuous marriage, an ambitious intruder who disrupts the child's succession to the father's place, a vow of revenge that is interminably delayed, the issue of castration, and a wasteland atmosphere of social decay. *Hamlet* focuses on the grief that the prince experiences over the separation from his mother. Like Tonio, Hamlet, upon his father's death, might have been able to look forward to a measure of oedipal fulfillment by having his mother to himself and enjoying the succession to the throne. However, Hamlet's uncle spoils the prince's expectations, just as Tonio's hopes are destroyed at the verge of their realization.

The early chapters of *Cry to Heaven* are constructed upon four oedipal triangles that involve only four members of the same family, three generations of males and a single female who is the object of desire for all the men. In the Treschi family, one of Venice's oldest, richest, and most powerful, the men vie both for the affections of Marianna—the wife of one, the mother of another, and the sister-wife of the third—and for the family legacy. Of course, the narrative focuses primarily upon the child Tonio, whose position within the four triangles shifts until he is displaced altogether. The initial family romance includes Tonio in the position of the oedipal child, his mother, Marianna, in the place of the desired object, and Andrea in the position of patriarch. This structure dissolves upon the death of Andrea. For a brief time, Tonio assumes the father's place and is in possession of the mother. The second triangle has its foundation in the union of mother and father-child. It is completed upon the return of Carlo, who is Tonio's actual father and ironically assumes the position of the oedipal child, contending for the mother and the estate, desiring nothing more than to displace Tonio from the position of authority. The third Freudian family structure arises from a shift in the position of two of the participants. The movement is precipitated when Marianna accepts Carlo as her lover, and Tonio learns that Carlo is his father and his brother. The oedipal conflict is exacerbated when Carlo has Tonio forcibly castrated and banished. The fourth triangle precedes the others chronologically, but within the narrative framework of the novel, it is exposed last. Before the action of the story began, Carlo defied Venetian and family law by seducing, impregnating, and choosing for a wife, Marianna, a woman who was not of aristocratic birth, an action that was a breach of class structure. As punishment, Andrea banished his son, but then he wed Marianna, whose condition he pitied. This situation constitutes an inversion of the traditional oedipal structure. The father takes possession of the son's potential bride, transforming her into the mother and then, figuratively, castrating the child with exile.

What Rice has produced in the early chapters of the novel is a family whose structural convolutions are so intricate as to constitute a virtual parody of the Freudian oedipal myth. The interpersonal turmoil of the family can, however, be traced back to a single incident: Andrea's banishment of his son and marriage to Marianna, the action that disrupted the traditional familial relations and perpetuates the family's suffering decades later. The ability of individuals to shift positions within the family reveals the destabilizing of traditional gender, filial, and fraternal categories. In *The Elementary Structure of Kinship*, anthropologist Claude Levi-Strauss delineated the importance of the "exchange of women" within the economy of social relations, indicating that the rules that govern this traffic solidify and validate cultural relations (24). In *Cry to Heaven*, both Andrea and Carlo have breached the dictates that police the exchange of women within the society, and their actions lead to the collapse of coherent family interaction. Indeed, the dissolution of the Treschi family is broadened to include an indictment of Venetian decadence. Tonio observes the association between his own family and the state itself. The shifting positions of family members suggest the Lacanian notion of the primacy of social and linguistic categories over life experience. Relations and subjectivity are determined by the individual's position in respect to the phallic signifier, not by metaphysics.

I must turn now to a closer examination of the oedipal relations of the Treschi family and show that these are Lacanian in nature. I will concentrate particularly on the two principal triangles: Andrea, Marianna, Tonio and Carlo, Marianna, Tonio.

The close relationship between Tonio and his mother is perhaps the most constant subject of the novel. Rice has taken great pains to indicate that their intimacy is atypical among mother-child relations. Understood in Lacanian terms, the relationship is representative of the mother-infant dyad in the mirror stage and is indicative of the resultant sense of wholeness and completion that characterizes this period in the life of the child. Of course, Lacan postulated this bonding within the first years of the child's development, prior to language acquisition. However, it is probably not logical for a writer to situate a story around the infancy of its central character, especially since the period is preverbal. In addition, the oedipal conflicts within the novel result from unresolved, reawakened familial tensions and can thus be expected to extend beyond the child's infancy.

Rice lends credibility to the mother-child intimacy, allowing for only a small gap in their ages. The mother is closer in age to her son than she is to her husband. Tonio recognizes that "she was much more the child than he was" (24). Thus, he adopts an unusual familiarity with her. The nature of their interpersonal relations shifts regularly, covering most of the traditional family interactions: mother and son, father and daughter, brother and sister, and husband and wife. Tonio takes responsibility for his mother's happiness because he perceives her to be neglected by her much older husband. The young man is invited by Andrea to accompany Marianna to the carnival where he looks after her as if he were her guardian. More and more, Andrea urges Tonio to take his (the father's) place in the mother's company, thus increasing the distance between husband and wife and encouraging the closure between mother and son. Indeed, Tonio recalls the first time that he ever saw Andrea treat her affectionately, an event that the reader is led to believe was quite uncommon. Andrea's commitment to the state of Venice keeps him from performing his conjugal duties with his wife, leaving her feeling lonely and abandoned. The reader later finds that Andrea had capitulated his conjugal duties altogether, acquiring a eunuch lover for his wife. In essence, these actions suggest the failure of the father to play his designated role of intercessor within the mother-infant bond.

Other facets of the mother-child relationship are indicative of an unusual intimacy. Tonio and his mother sleep in the same bed, and often their embraces border on the erotic, at least for the child:

> Yet as soon as she opened her arms, he flew into her lap and lay against her breast as still as if he were dead, one arm around her neck, the other hand clutching her shoulder so tightly he was hurting her. She was little more than a girl herself, but he didn't

know it. He felt her lips on his cheek, on his hair. He melted into her gentleness [10].

The intermittent disputes and reconciliations that punctuate the relationship suggest the vicissitudes of a romance. The above embrace is a sign of the mother's remorse after a period of cruelty toward the child. Tonio and Marianna share an especially intimate bond through their singing. In a novel where singing is consistently associated with ecstasy, both spiritual and physical, the duets sung by mother and child imply a romantic union. Of course, I do not mean to suggest that Marianna and her child actually share sexual intimacy. I mean only that the oedipal longings of the child are more fully realized for Tonio than for most children because of the absence of his father.

Tonio experiences the obligatory jealousies of the oedipal child toward the objects of his mother's affections. The Lacanian child wishes to became the focus of his mother's desire, to take the place of her lover— namely, the father. Tonio fantasizes about becoming his mother's "cavalier servante" and becomes bitterly envious when he perceives that a man, accompanying his cousin Catrina, has become too familiar with his mother: "He felt a hot and agonizing jealousy. No man had ever been close to her save Tonio" (26). When Tonio and his mother attend the carnival together, he sees her kissing an unknown masker. Troubled, he inquires into her behavior, but she denies any impropriety (69–70). Most important, the boy dreams of taking Andrea's place and subsequently rehabilitating his mother and his own childhood. When he tries to envision his future wife, the names and faces of cousins are replaced by the image of his mother, whom he sees laughing and accompanying him to "great balls" and to the family "villa on the Brenta" (34). He sees her as the bearer of his children whose perfect lives would amend his own. Tonio's fantasy of union with his mother may not be as simply Freudian as it seems. Lacan maintains that the traumatic separation from the mother initiates the child's erotic desires, longings that can never fully satisfy the child because they can never actually replace the mirror-stage union. The child is left feeling incomplete, each object of his affection falling short of his desire for his mother. Lacan termed these mother surrogates the "objet à" (Lee 179–80). The structure of Tonio's dream does not necessarily involve a literal maternal union. He begins by wondering, "Who would be his wife?" (34). Tonio does not harbor a delusional belief that he can marry his mother. He first considers the "names and faces of cousins" (34) who are the realistic conjugal prospects, but then he goes on to indicate that they cannot compensate for the loss of Marianna, a particularly apt allusion to the Lacanian fragmented subject who remains incomplete as a result of language and the oedipal trauma.

Tonio's father, Andrea, goes beyond the image of the Freudian super-ego. He is a literal representation of the Venetian state, possessing a public life from which the son and the wife are excluded. He is language, law, and order, the figuration of the Lacanian phallus. He is the power that sets the boundaries of the child's desire, the focal point of reference at which the endless differentiation of language signification begins. Through Andrea's name (the Name-of-the-Father)—Treschi—Tonio learns his identity and his place within the social order. Tonio's obedience to the law of the father constitutes a separation from the mother. Unlike his brother-father before him, Tonio knows that he must marry and propagate according to the Venetian family traditions to take his place at the head of the state and of the family. Tonio longs for that place. His admiration for Andrea's aristocratic position reveals the boy's longing. Rice clearly portrays mother and father as occupying distinctly different realms of human activity. Marianna is domestic and private, and Andrea is public. Tonio is thrilled with his father's public persona. He recalls that when he was taken to church as a young boy, he saw Andrea parade pompously down the aisle with the other members of the Grand Council of the Venetian State. The boy experiences a special exhilaration when his father acknowledges him with a smile, a gesture of warmth transcending the man's austerity. Tonio later reflects upon Andrea as the literal representation of the law, "more powerful than Doge himself" (15). Andrea, who was elected to the "Council of Three, that awesome triumvirate of inquisitors" (15), possessed the power of life and death. The idealization of the father's power is perhaps representative of the Lacanian phallus. Tonio's desire to take the father's place suggests his belief that he can obtain the phallus, the unobtainable wholeness. Such a view is both a revelation of his naiveté and a delusion that the events of his life will dispel.

Tonio reflects upon his future as one of the pillars of the Venetian state, acknowledging that even the Doge was not beyond his aspiration or his grasp (19). At the same time, he perceives the state to be in decline, and when his father falls sick, he associates the incident with Venetian decadence (59). Perhaps this signals the beginning of the child's recognition that the power represented by the phallus is unobtainable, and in reality, is only an idealization. However, the boy has yet to fully internalize such a lesson. More and more, Tonio begins to take Andrea's place at public functions. He is the sole heir to the Treschi fortune, and when Andrea dies, it appears as if he may attain the oedipal child's fantasy: possession of the mother and usurpation of the father.

However, the father's death brings the unexpected return of Carlo from banishment.

Although Tonio had learned of Carlo's existence before the demise of Andrea, he has not yet learned the full story of Carlo's exile, nor is he aware of his true relationship to the man. The terms of Tonio's succession to preeminence in the family and the state are quite rigid; even he is not in a position to subvert them. He is the beneficiary of Andrea's estate unless he should prove unable to conceive children, a requirement intended to perpetuate a family that has been among Venice's most influential for centuries. For a time, Tonio has no trouble fulfilling the obligations of his position, but more and more, Carlo regains his former standing within the Venetian state, displacing Tonio. Although Carlo is at first respectful of, and even obliging toward, his brother, he becomes increasingly more assertive until he openly challenges Tonio, asking him to step aside. Carlo explains that he was unreasonably banished and dispossessed by his father because he loved Marianna, who was not a member of Venice's affluent families and therefore was not a suitable wife. Carlo had pleaded with his father to buy Marianna into the Golden Book of Venetian families, but Andrea refused, stating that such an action was outside of his authority. However, once Carlo was sent away, Andrea took Marianna as his own wife and, upon learning that she was pregnant with Carlo's child, raised the boy as his own. Thus, Tonio learns that Andrea was actually his grandfather and that Carlo is his real father. Carlo complains that Andrea stole his wife and child and banished him from Venice. He adds that he has returned after many years only to find himself "slain" (96). Carlo, of course, refers to his displacement from his birthright. He has been succeeded by his son before his own death.

The stunning revelations awaken Tonio's formerly resolved oedipal conflicts. He occupies the position of authority, but he begins to withdraw, relying more upon his conviction that Andrea's will cannot be subverted than upon any legitimate right that he may have to the Treschi estate. Given the young man's behavior, it is possible to believe that he would have resigned his place if he were not bound by Andrea's legacy and Venetian law. His sphere of activities becomes smaller and Carlo's becomes larger. Once again, he has a rival for his mother's affections. The return of his real father arouses dormant jealousies. As Carlo and Marianna rekindle their love, Tonio begins acting like a spurned lover. He bursts into his mother's chambers, expecting to find Carlo there. His father-brother reminds him that Marianna is a sensuous woman who has been deprived of male company for years and that she will not be content to live in her child's house as a "grieving widow." Tonio protests that

Marianna was Carlo's "father's wife" (103–6). Only after Marianna admits her desire to accept Carlo as her lover does Tonio concede defeat: "His mother was somewhere lost to him behind closed doors" (123).

Lacan asserts that all longing is the desire for recognition, specifically from the mother through the mother replacement: "[T]he first desire of any human is the absolute one for recognition (the Desire to be desired), itself linked to the Desire to be a unity" (Ragland-Sullivan 58). Because Tonio does not seriously expect to consummate his desire for his mother, his ambition is to be acknowledged as the most important person in her life. After he bursts into her chamber unexpectedly, he makes her admit that she "stands with him" (113). However, once he recognizes that he cannot displace Carlo from her affections, he abandons the Treschi estate and begins to console himself among the Venetian prostitutes, one of whom is older than Marianna. The prostitutes become replacements for the mother, replacements that can never restore the lost wholeness of the mother-infant dyad. He capitulates his place within the household and goes to the brothels of Venice, sulking and leaving the spoils of victory to his father.

He receives news from his cousin Catrina that Carlo has taken over the house and has begun restoring the family property as if it were his own (110). Even before his literal castration by Carlo's ruffians, Tonio has already been emasculated in the Lacanian sense. Carlo has broken the mother-infant bond, forcing the child out of the house and into the public arena. The family romantic triangle has once again shifted. Although Tonio still retains the Name-of-the-Father, Carlo has assumed all of the authority therein and has become, for Tonio, the figuration of the phallus, returning the younger man to the position of the spurned child. However, instead of beginning to identify with the father as is the case in the post-oedipal phase, Tonio despises Carlo and does not accept his authority. Because Tonio does not make a complete capitulation to his father-brother or surrender the Name-of-the-Father, Carlo rationalizes his removal.

Thus far, I have ignored that part of the story that most readers consider its principal subject matter: Tonio's voice. Although it is inappropriate for the son and heir of a Venetian patrician to perform in front of a crowd, Tonio enjoys showing off his prepubescent voice, often in duet with his mother. Carlo learns that Tonio sang for Guido Maffeo, a eunuch and a former opera singer whose own voice was ruined and who is now searching for talent for the musical conservatory of Naples, an institution whose function is to train the voices of castrati youth. Carlo engineers a plan to remove his son without killing him. Since Tonio's authority within the family rests upon his ability to procreate, his castration would deprive him of the family legacy and eliminate him as Carlo's rival. Moreover, Carlo gambles that Tonio will not reveal the crime against him to the Venetian authorities because of the boy's loyalty to the family. When the Lacanian oedipal child capitulates his bond with the mother, his compensation is the identity that the Name-of-the-Father confers. To kill the father would be to destroy the source of the child's own identity (Lee 65). Thus, when Carlo hires a group of thugs to carry out the plan and deliver the emasculated boy to the reluctant and fearful Guido Maffeo, Tonio does nothing until he is sure that Carlo has secured the family line. If Tonio revealed his father's crime, he would eliminate the last virile male of the Treschi name, and the family that has endured for centuries would die. Paradoxically, Carlo exploits Tonio's allegiance to remove him from the family, and it is Carlo's own indifference to the family's future that permits him to assume its leadership.

If one views Carlo's actions from the Freudian perspective, they assume an entirely different emphasis. Tonio's condition is a literalization of the Freudian castration complex. The oedipal boy is compelled to abandon his incestuous desire for his mother out of fear that the father will castrate him. This separation leads the boy toward an eventual identification with the father. The process is necessary in the construction of gender and in the child's socialization. Carlo's action does indeed force Tonio out of the womblike security of the Treschi family and into the world of human relations, where he must employ all of his talents and abilities to succeed. He temporarily deprives his son of an identity, and although we see Tonio suffer greatly, it is difficult to conclude that he would have been a better person had he never gone under the knife. Thus, Rice has created an interesting ethical dilemma, one that is not easily resolved. Of course, it is important to remember that the Freudian child is not actually castrated, but he is forced out of competition with the father by the fear of castration. The more appropriate model for the boy's experience is Lacan's theory, in which every child is castrated twice—once by the father and once by language.

Tonio's castration occurs shortly after his realization that he has lost his mother to his father-brother and after he has already begun to surrender his public persona by withdrawing into the Venetian brothels. Thus, his emasculation can be viewed as both literal and figurative. The oedipal child resolves his conflicts only by "giving up his claim to be the Phallus, the imaginary object of the [m]Other's desire." The traumatic loss, however, necessitates a prolonged period of mourning (Lee 111). Tonio has surrendered the phallus to his brother-father, and the period immediately following his arrival in Naples constitutes his time of mourning.

Only his self-loathing exceeds the contempt that he feels for Carlo. He refers to eunuchs as "things" rather than as men, and he calls himself a "monster" (161–62). He adds that "I am some creature whose name I cannot speak" (247). Interestingly, the phrasing of his statement encourages a dual reading. Ostensibly, the name that he cannot speak is "eunuch," but it is also the name "Treschi," the Name-of-the-Father. The loss of his testicles is the loss of his identity and his position within the state, the family, and gender distinctions. He no longer occupies a place within the symbolic order. "Eunuch" does not signify any coherent gender category. He complains, "I am neither man nor woman" (246). The absence of the phallus constitutes the loss of language. The phallus was the signifier that initiated the child's first encounter with the symbolic. The post-oedipal child defines himself in relationship to the phallus, a distinction that initiates the oppositions that generate meaning. The first meaning for the child is gender, and Tonio is neither. In Lacanian psychoanalytic theory, Tonio's predicament suggests the universal castration, the sense of fragmentation and emptiness that follows the child's separation from the mother. Secondary castration is related to the subject's inability to place himself fully into language, to represent the self accurately. Indeed, when the Lacanian subject speaks the name "I," he fictionalizes himself, constructing a self out of the preexisting categories of language into which he does not fit (Ragland-Sullivan 7–16).

Tonio refuses to account for the multiple significations of the term "man." He does not realize that to speak the word "eunuch" is also to speak the word "man," and that in Lacanian psychoanalysis, to speak the word "man" is also to say "eunuch," the general condition of all humanity. Tonio believes in a single ideal image of manhood:

> A man. He smiled at the brutal simplicity of that word and its great avalanche of meanings. And for the first time in his life the word struck him as … as what? Coarse. Never mind. You deceive yourself, he half whispered aloud. For all its vast abstraction, the word had but one fully understood meaning [253].

In the course of his education as a eunuch, Tonio must recognize that the idealized concept of male potency signifies an unreal category; the boundaries of "man" are unstable. For Tonio, "man" or the phallus is represented by his father, whose power and influence threaten to overwhelm him. In relationship to this idealization of the phallus, Tonio can never again feel like a "whole man." He cannot accept the failure of language or refuse the "metaphysics of presence." Tonio's recognition that he will never possess the phallus (in all of Lacan's significations) creates the sense of fragmentation that the Lacanian subject forever tries to repair.

The first sign of Tonio's despair is his rebellion against the regulations of the conservatory. Upon his arrival, he refuses to sing, suggesting that to do so would be to accept the consequences of his father's base designs. He refuses to wear the standard uniform of the castrati student, a black robe with a red sash, because he does not want to exhibit his difference and make himself the object of mockery by "whole men." The uniform would confer upon him an unacceptable identity. He also becomes belligerent toward the other students, perhaps despising them because of his resemblance to them; this aspect of his aggression leads ultimately to a bar fight in which he is forced to kill another eunuch. Eventually, Tonio is thrown out of the conservatory. However, with the opportunity to reflect upon his predicament, he returns because he has no other place to go. His family refuses to support him unless he remains at the school. Whether he returns out of sheer frustration and exhaustion or because he has already formulated a plot to execute his revenge upon Carlo is unclear at this point.

Even after he decides to cooperate with Guido's instruction, Tonio still refuses to live the life that is traditionally associated with the castrati. He keeps the company of "whole men," learning to fence because he will one day employ his skills against his father and because the practice is not characteristic of the activities of the castrati. He refuses to accept the socially constituted role of the eunuch, desiring to show that he can still compete with men whom he secretly regards as superior to himself. His accomplishments in fencing become notorious; the other swordsmen fear offending him. However, when these men make a gesture of friendship toward Tonio by inviting him to accompany them on an outing, the eunuch refuses to attend. These men represent that idealized manhood that Tonio believes that he cannot attain.

Another arena in which Tonio attempts to work out his sense of fragmentation is in the bedroom. This perhaps constitutes the greatest challenge for him in the reformulation of his self-image. For a long time, he is unwilling to sleep with a woman despite the fact that the women of the novel find eunuchs irresistible. He chooses instead to sleep with the most effeminate castrati. He exploits Domenico as he would a prostitute, using him sexually but refusing to support him emotionally. Indeed, Tonio's movement toward sexual openness is parallel to his development as a singer, and it is perhaps just as important in understanding the structure of the central portions of the novel. Gradually, Tonio seems to accept his androgyny, a movement most clearly represented in his partners, who become increasingly representative of male aggression and potency. This culminates in his rape by Count di Stephano.

Tonio's numerous encounters with men raise questions about his sexual identity. His shift from the love of women to the love of men may be merely a matter of convenience. There are many androgynous castrati boys in the school. They are portrayed as possessing a female charm that could attract Tonio as other men are later attracted to him, but this theory does not explain the increasing masculinity of Tonio's partners and his increasing surrender to them. Perhaps his failure to engage sexually with women results from fear of sexual inadequacy, a concern that a female partner would be repulsed by his condition. Under these circumstances, sex with other castrati would be safe because they possess the same physical condition. This hypothesis does not explain how he could later copulate with normal males, among whom his sense of inadequacy would be much greater than among women who do not possess a penis themselves. Neither does it account for the fact that women show an intense sexual desire for him despite his castration. An additional problem with this reading is that it perpetuates a regressive-repressive view of homosexuals as ruined heterosexuals, and it classifies homosexuality itself as a pathology.

Still another view of Tonio's alteration negates the idea of transformation altogether. I refer to Freud's theory of the polymorphous perverse, a condition that characterizes all infants and is latent in everyone's nature. The individual sexual subject moves from an unfocused bisexuality in infancy to a narrower field of sexual objects, characterized as heterosexuality or homosexuality. Therefore, "one does not become a pervert, but remains one" (Dollimore 172). Thus, Tonio experiences an awakening of his latent bisexuality once his castration lifts the demands of socially constituted gender categories. Certainly this reading is consistent with the idea of sexual freedom that is so prevalent within the novel. Gender construction that emphasized obligatory heterosexuality may have been even more powerful in Tonio's social conditioning than in the average child's because it was imperative that he procreate to continue the family dynasty.

The vexed Freudian theory of penis envy can also illuminate Tonio's sexuality. Freud maintained that the female oedipal child experiences a disappointment over her failure to possess what society has deemed the preferred sexual organ: the penis. She thus begins to resent her mother, who is also bereft of the male organ and whom the girl blames for her own loss. Eventually, she begins to compensate for the perceived absence by desiring the penis of the father and, later, of father replacements. Perhaps Rice is subtly ridiculing the phallocentric disposition of Freudian theory by portraying a castrated male who experiences penis envy and begins to desire the sexual organ that he possesses only in part. This would certainly explain Tonio's initial aggression when he arrives at the conservatory.

Freud also suggested that homosexuality may result when the father is absent from the home or is not a fit subject for the male child's emulation, causing the male child to closely identify with the mother (Dollimore 197). This theory is viable within the context of the novel because Tonio does indeed identify with his mother, and once Andrea dies, Tonio has no father figure to emulate until, of course, he arrives at the conservatory. Perhaps his numerous male lovers comprise his search for a father. Of course, principal among them would be Guido, who is a figure of severity and authority, but also of love. After his castration, Tonio is delivered into Guido's hands. It becomes Guido's duty to nurture his growth both as a singer and as a person. He teaches Tonio about their physical condition, outlining the numerous transformations that the boy's body will undergo as a result of his castration. Indeed, he helps Tonio resolve the problems surrounding the ambiguity of his gender. Paradoxically, the resolution constitutes an absence of closure. He advises Tonio that the castrati are neither gender and are, therefore, not bound by the socially constituted gender roles. The development of Tonio's voice is directly parallel to the process of his mourning. By the time that he is ready to sing in the Roman opera, he has at least superficially come to terms with his castration. It is Guido who, like a father, has nurtured this acceptance. The significant breakthrough for Tonio occurs when he discovers that Guido has harbored a sincere romantic affection for him. For Tonio, Guido represents a rehabilitation of the most vexed relationship in the boy's socialization. Guido becomes father, brother, and lover. The great injury that Tonio received at the hands of his father-brother is symbolically redeemed through Guido's love and acceptance. The most significant breakthrough in Tonio's interpersonal relations following his castration comes after he surrenders to Guido. He has to learn that he is not self-sufficient and that he must trust others.

The progress of Tonio's revised socialization becomes a process of feminization. Tonio becomes increasingly more androgynous. By the time that he leaves Naples to sing in the Roman opera, Tonio is already playing the wife to Guido's husband. Indeed, the addition of the boy Paolo to the couple completes the triangulation of the queer family. There are, however, no signs of oedipal conflict here. This sexually liberated family possesses none of the tensions of the traditional domestic unit. In a display of maternal affection, Tonio invites Paolo to accompany them to Rome because he cannot stand to think of the unhappiness that the boy will experience once they are gone. Fidelity, however, is not an obligatory attribute of the eunuch family, and Tonio becomes involved with other men, gradually assuming a feminine role. In his relationship with the cardinal, he is wooed, exploited sexually, and dismissed, just as a woman might be by a powerful man of the eighteenth century. Eventually, the cardinal's guilt over the affair becomes too great to endure, but he admits that he cannot account for Tonio in his metaphysical system. The cardinal cannot condemn Tonio outright as an unnatural creature, yet he believes that Tonio has an evil effect on him and would consign his soul to damnation (398–400). It is after his encounters with the cardinal that Tonio agrees to impersonate a woman onstage, a role that he had previously resisted. In his next encounter, he is ravished by a lascivious count, who afterward becomes his benefactor. Of course, this process continues to the end of the novel, at which time, in the guise of a woman, he seduces his own father.

There are essentialist and social-constructionist arguments for Tonio's behavioral transformation. From the former point of view, Tonio's increasing androgynous behavior results from the physiological effects of his castration. Thus, his actions are biologically determined, perhaps stemming from decreased levels of testosterone in his body. The crime against him transforms his very nature. From the social-constructionist perspective, Tonio becomes more androgynous because "whole men" treat him as an object of desire, thrusting him into the feminine role. The latter perspective is closest to a Lacanian explanation. For Lacan, identity and meaning are determined solely by the place of the subject within the signifying chain. Consistent with the binary thinking within the novel, Tonio must be feminine if he is not masculine. Thus, men treat him as such, and he conforms his behavior accordingly. He finds himself in the position of the desired object, the final position of the family triangle, and he adopts the behaviors that are associated with that role. A third explanation for Tonio's androgyny is that it is all a ruse, a calculated preparation for his impending confrontation with his father. Paradoxically, his femininity serves the interests of his masculine agenda. It is a masquerade, a carnivalesque abandonment that is intended to restore and maintain the order that his castration breached.

Tonio's behavioral change, however, is more involved than I have previously suggested. Tonio's obsession over his mother does not subside after his forced castration and banishment. Indeed, it is accompanied by the sense of betrayal common to the post-oedipal child who feels that his mother has turned against him by embracing the father. Tonio does not, however, blame his mother for the physical injury perpetrated against him. As a matter of fact, he assumes that she does not, or will not, know that Carlo was behind the incident. Moreover, he continues to show concern for her, delaying his revenge on Carlo because he does not want to kill the father of his mother's two young children (484). In the absence of the desired mother, Tonio transfers his affections onto himself. Freud theorized that homosexuality was essentially narcissistic; the subject loves the self in the same way that the mother loved him (Ragland-Sullivan 31). Tonio becomes his mother by gradually creating a representation of the androgynous whole that was a part of the mirror-stage union of mother and child. Instead of following the path of the spurned post-oedipal child and identifying with the father to become the normative, male, sexual subject, Tonio regards his mother as both the object of sexual desire and the role model for sexual socialization. He physically and ideologically becomes male and female.

In his encounters with men, Tonio reenacts his mother's sexual history. In his relationship with the cardinal, he imitates his mother's marriage to Andrea. Both men are the representations of the phallic order, and both relationships are passionless unions between older, powerful men and young sex objects. Tonio's experience with Count di Stephano reenacts his mother's bond with Carlo. Both men are young, virile, and roguish. The forced encounter between Tonio and di Stephano is reminiscent of the deflowering of Marianna by Carlo before his banishment, and it is perhaps a preparation for the final encounter with his father. With di Stephano, Tonio learns of the erotic power that he exercises over "whole men," a power that he and his mother shared and one that he will use to bring his father under his control.

Paradoxically, Tonio's re-creation of his mother's sexual history results in the attainment of the father and in the acquisition of the [m]Other. It is after Tonio has achieved a full androgyny that he is once again able to consummate his desire for a woman. Tonio's union with Christina represents the revival of the mirror stage fusion with the mother and the sense of wholeness, ecstasy and power that coincides with that bond (Roberts "Historical Novels" 208). Two mirror images accompany the culmination of Tonio's gender reconstruction. When he completes his makeup and costume preparation for his first night in the Roman opera, he experiences an imaginary confrontation:

> When he rose and turned to the mirror, he felt that familiar and
> no less alarming loss. Where was Tonio in this hourglass of dark

red satin? Where was the boy behind these darkly painted eyes, these rouged lips, and this flowing white hair...?

It seemed he was drifting as he stared at her in the glass, and she whispered his name to him, and then drew back like some phantom on the other side who might suddenly take life away from him as he himself stood still [410].

The female who appears in the mirror is his interior [m]Other, who bestows upon him a new identity by whispering his name. Unless it is the father's name that she whispers, this constitutes a deliberate inversion of the Lacanian axiom that identity is derived through the Name-of-the-Father. Indeed, Tonio has refused to take the customary stage name for his performance. He insists on using his family name, Treschi, a decision that suggests his reinstatement within the phallic order, a new sense of identity derived from a renewed power.

In the second mirror image, Tonio is again accompanied by a female, this time the mother replacement, Christina. Once again, there is a merging of two images in the mirror, suggesting the unity of the mother-infant dyad:

He closed his eyes. The mirror was gone, and so were the garments that covered both of them; or so it seemed to him. And he was thinking dreamily again of how he'd liked as a child to be invisible in the dark.... And in the mirror saw that shimmering vision of the two of them, lost in disguises, but a perfect pair [473].

Tonio imagines the literal bonding of the self and the [m]Other, represented by Christina. The ecstatic nature of the union is related to the sense of completion that the infant experiences in the relevant stage of psychic development.

Tonio's bond with Christina resembles a rehabilitation and idealization of his relationship with his mother. Christina is an androgynous, independent woman who is not a slave to gender stereotypes; she does as she pleases. When she chooses to become lovers with a eunuch, she does not concern herself with social prohibitions. Thus, she redeems the tragic vulnerability of Marianna, who was objectified and manipulated by the men of the novel. Marianna dies tormented with regret that she has chosen wrongly between Carlo and Tonio; she dies whispering Tonio's name. One of the principal moments of mother-child bonding between Tonio and Marianna is reiterated in the relationship between Tonio and

Christina. Just as in Venice, Tonio accompanies a woman to the carnival. This time, the companion is Christina rather than his mother, but both situations are indicative of Tonio's public coming out, his assumption of his father's name, and his rehabilitated phallic power. In Lacanian terms, Tonio's voice becomes a compensation for the fragmentation of the ego that results from literal and symbolic castration. It becomes a replacement for the phallus, the representation of power and influence. Many signs of Tonio's maturation accompany his success as a singer. He insists upon using his family name rather than a customary stage name. He agrees to impersonate a woman when onstage. He continues his androgynous role in the bedroom. He regains his ability to consummate his affection for a woman.

Tonio attends the carnival with Christina in a celebration of his recent successes. However, the attempted assassination of the singer by his father's hired thugs mars the event. This is a reiteration of the father's original intervention in the mother-infant union. However, men who have been hired by Cardinal Calvino to protect Tonio foil the attempt. These events revise the catastrophe of Tonio's castration and displacement. The paid servants of the cardinal, the representation of the power structure, rescue Tonio from the aggression of Carlo, thus pointing out the failure of Venetian authorities to fulfill their obligations to the young man when he was heir to the Treschi name. Moreover, the cardinal has already been portrayed as the resurrection of the phallic power of Andrea, the father whose name Tonio was to assume. These events immediately follow Tonio's resumption of the father's name on the Roman stage. In these actions, the failures of the family and state are redeemed.

Carlo's most recent affront resuscitates the oedipal aggressions that the son had virtually resolved, making it necessary for Tonio to assume an offensive stance against his father's aggression to assure his own safety and happiness. The failure of the assassination attempt is a sign of the failing influence of the father and the empowerment of the son, who uses the advantages of androgyny to seduce and entrap Carlo. Dressed as a Venetian prostitute, Tonio lures his drunken father away from the protection of his bodyguards to an abandoned room, where he binds Carlo and then doffs and burns his disguise.

The father's original blunder was his assumption that he could eliminate his son as a rival if he emasculated him. It was a faith in the binary thinking of gender stereotypes. If the son was not a virile male, he was a female with all of the characteristics of the eighteenth century's construction of femininity. However, the father begins to recognize his mistake before the return of Tonio to Venice, and his decision to send his assassins against Tonio is an indication of this awareness. He expected the emasculation of Tonio to make the boy "meek and diffident" (513). But Tonio's history as a eunuch teaches Carlo the limitations of binary thought and the failure of language to fully account for humanity. Tonio refused to live like the traditional eunuch, and Carlo came to believe that Tonio's every action was a calculated effort to defeat and humiliate him. He believes that Tonio lived his life to "torment" him (512). Instead of turning his son into a woman, he armed the young man with redoubled strength, the strength of both genders.

Carlo still tries to convince himself that he is safe even though his efforts to kill Tonio reveal his paranoia. When the narration returns to Venice at the end of the novel, Carlo is shown drunken and broken in the city square, attempting to convince himself that he is safe from his son's revenge. The father that Tonio encounters is not the representation of power and law, the Name-of-the-Father. Carlo never attained the power he hoped for as the head of the Treschi house. The phallus was just an illusion. His relationship with Marianna failed; in her final days, she turned with longing for her son. Moreover, Carlo failed to gain peace of mind as a head of state. He bitterly complains that power is ultimately unrewarding, and he tries to convince Tonio that the young man was fortunate to avoid the burden.

The final confrontation between Tonio and Carlo is a parody of the post-oedipal stage of the psychological development in which the male child experiences a "homoerotic identification with the father, a position of feminized subordination to the father as a condition of finding a model for his own hetero role" (Sedgewick 23). Tonio seduces his father to bring the man under his power. This constitutes an inversion of normative, post-oedipal relations. Here, the son employs femininity to defeat, not to capitulate and emulate. Moreover, as the previous chapters show, Tonio's homoerotic experiences are not a transitory stage. He first obtains the symbolic father and then defeats the real one. His resulting sexual predisposition is toward bisexuality and androgyny, as is illustrated at the end of the novel when Tonio rejoins both Guido and Christina, the two halves of his divided self. In that image, he has assumed the third and final place in the oedipal triangle, the place of the mother, the focus of desire. However, by possessing both the male and the female attributes, he has transformed the category. Tonio, unlike his mother, is not the helpless victim of the competition between dominant males. He thus redeems both genders by feminizing the male and masculinizing the female.

Tonio's return to Venice reveals yet another significant character transformation. He has learned Hamlet's lesson: the necessity of guile. When Tonio left Venice, he was a naive boy who had allowed himself to be circumvented by his father's deceit. Upon his return, he employs that same deceit not to win his birthright, but to achieve his safety. This idea is most fully realized in his use of disguise to bring his father under his control, but his guile goes beyond masks. He now understands the deceitful mind. He can penetrate his father's treachery, and when he offers a reconciliation and his father ostensibly accepts, he knows better than to trust the man. He prepares himself for more cunning. Once loosed from his bonds, Carlo attacks Tonio, and Tonio must kill his father.

In the final image of the novel, Tonio rejoins both Guido and Christina, forming a love triangle that recuperates the crises and rivalries of the Treschi family romances. Tonio has attained the final position in the oedipal structure, the focus of desire for the other members of the triangle, the mother's place. The image of androgyny is perhaps the wholeness that Lacan says we are striving all our lives to regain without success. The mother is attained because the mother is internalized.

Many aspects of Rice's portrayal of eighteenth-century eunuchs seem revolutionary. On the surface, the conclusion of the novel promotes a very progressive agenda, the value of androgyny, that seems to deconstruct gender categories, collapsing the binary opposition upon which gender hierarchy is constructed. However, we must remember that Tonio burns his dress in front of his father while the father is bound in the chair. Such an act suggests the repudiation of the feminine, a vindictive display of Tonio's refusal to accept the sexual subordination that his father imposed upon him. We discover that what seemed to be Tonio's growing acquiescence to his physical condition has actually been a means to an end. Many of his concessions have been calculated to prepare him for his final confrontation with his father. His sudden decision to portray a woman at the Roman opera, after so much resistance to the role, indicates an ulterior motive, and a portion of his erotic encounters with men seems crafted to test and perfect his powers of seduction. In this context, much of Tonio's androgyny is a ruse. If the burning of the dress signifies the rejection of his female mask, then Tonio could be said to be reasserting the traditional gender hierarchy, which holds that the masculine is superior to the feminine and that the feminine must be repressed. If the lesson that Tonio teaches his father is that one does not make a man into a woman by castrating him, Tonio is not undermining patriarchal values. Instead, he is reinforcing them, indicating that the feminine is something to be overcome.

If a substantial portion of Tonio's actions can be attributed to his desire for power and revenge, than how does he deviate from mainstream masculine values? He has subordinated his female attributes to the masculine will and, therefore, left the patriarchy intact. Just as the women are used in the novel to attain power (to acquire Marianna was to attain the Name-of-the-Father), Tonio's feminine attributes are exploited to advance his masculine goals and desires. Tonio has internalized the socially and historically constituted predisposition toward the masculine. When he is placed in a position where it is socially acceptable and even encouraged to impersonate a woman, he can do so only to promote a male agenda: revenge and power. In his decision to play the role of a woman in the opera, Tonio uses his female characteristics, his appearance and voice, to win glory and influence, to become famous and admired, a position in the eighteenth century that was generally reserved for males. We need only remember that the eunuch himself is as much a repudiation of the feminine as the masculine. A castrati singer is, after all, an imperfect replacement for a woman on the stage, a privileged space where society had forbidden women to intrude. So the castrati are the very emblem of the patriarchy's effort to usurp the power of women and employ it for masculine goals.

Many of the theories for the origin of Tonio's homosexuality that can be generated by the text are heterosexist and patriarchal. They link homosexuality with the disruption of the normative heterosexual function. In the novel, the young man's sexual identity is a consequence of his castration. He pursues a conventional eroticism until his injury. If everything had gone well for Tonio, he would have had a traditional sex life. From this position, homoeroticism is the pursuit of half-men, men so broken that they cannot function adequately. Such theories pathologize alternative sexual practices. Moreover, within the novel, Tonio cannot be said to have recovered from the emotional trauma of his injury until he has resumed his former heterosexual practices. All of these implications equate homosexuality with abnormal psychology, a condition to be overcome if one is to lead a truly gratifying life. Moreover, the cardinal's rejection of Tonio reinforces the repressive religious strictures against same-sex relations. The cardinal's ambivalence toward Tonio fortifies the tradition of persecution and exclusion of homosexuals by the church.

Rice also subverts Lacan's radical theories of human subjectivity. Lacan postulated the fragmentation of the human ego. The subject, constructed out of language, can never fully understand itself because it can never be clearly observed through language. There is no metalanguage with which to gain analytical perspective of the language that generates human subjectivity (Ragland-Sullivan 233). The self cannot know the self. Rice seems to pursue this line of inquiry through much of the novel, but in the final chapters she reasserts self-knowledge, which is possible through the acquaintance of the subject with the internal parents. The individual can achieve wholeness if she discovers the androgynous self, the other within. The novel implies that such a self is knowable. Thus, the result is a very conventional notion of human subjectivity.

In its family politics, the novel fails to achieve a progressive agenda as well. Lacan's theories postulate a family fraught with sexual tensions and rivalries, an institution that is a universal failure at preparing the child for a fulfilling life. It initiates most of the pathologies that a child will manifest in her lifetime and leaves the child so empty that she must strive futilely to regain the sense of wholeness that was lost in infancy. Yet Rice's novel, after all the suffering and destruction, reasserts the family structure, even offering it as a paradigm for the eunuch relationship, with a few telling differences of course. Indeed, it imposes the heterosexist relational structure onto alternative lifestyles as if it were the appropriate model for all people despite their sexual predispositions. The homosexual-eunuch family (Guido, Tonio, Paolo) is modeled on the traditional family unit of husband, wife, and child. In this context, the relationships within the eunuch family are degraded through comparison to the normative family, which is held up as the paradigm for emulation. The inherent sterility of the relationship reinforces this denigration. The bond that does not prove fruitful is inferior to the bond that does, especially if the goal of the former bond is the same as the latter. If the homosexual couple desires children but is unable to produce them, then that relationship must be inferior to the coupling that has the same goal and is able to achieve it. Although Rice attempts to portray the eunuch family as normative, she only succeeds in making it seem inferior and unnatural because she attempts to force it into a pattern that it does not fit. She reinforces the ideology of the traditional family at the same time that she tries to overthrow it.

The conservative subtext of Rice's family politics is also reflected in the origins and resolution of the Treschi family's conflicts. The problems in the family began when Carlo breached Venetian marriage traditions and Andrea exceeded the bounds of paternal authority by buying Marianna into the Golden Book and laying claim to her as his wife. Thus, all of the trouble derives from two fractures of Venetian class structure and two violations of family structure. The implication is that if social institutions had prevailed over individual will, tragedy might have been avoided. The disorder that the actions of Carlo and Andrea wrought is only resolved after Carlo pays the price of his ambition, like the scapegoat who regenerates the wasteland. At the end of the novel, there is a conventional resolution that restores the structure of family and state. Ironically, Tonio, the sexual revolutionary, is a conservative force bringing about the reinstatement of the old order, paving the way for Carlo's child to continue the Treschi dynasty unchanged.

Chapter 4

VIOLATION
AND SEX EDUCATION:
BEAUTY'S EROTIC ODYSSEY

The uproar over televising Ellen DeGeneres' coming out had the corruption of children as its referent. The complaint hurled at the show's producers involved the time slot in which the episode was aired; it was a time when one might expect a significant number of child viewers. Of course, those who oppose the depiction of such subjects on television could have been relied upon to invent other objections had the show been aired later in the evening. Yet the appeal to the child's innocence is frequently the most moving protest, particularly when the objectionable subject is homosexuality, because the complaint perpetuates the myth of recruitment through which America's parents attempt to disavow their own potential responsibility for their child's homosexuality by blaming it on the predacious behavior of a complete stranger or the media. From this perspective, DeGeneres' coming out is not an expression of her identity, but it is a tool for the enlisting of a host of queer neophytes who somehow would have remained ignorant of the possibility for same-sex eroticism had they not been tutored in the lifestyle by a situation comedy. Indeed, this desire to keep children innocent involves the effort to keep children ignorant of sexual possibilities. Our culture defines the line between child and adult and between innocence and corruption in terms of sexual awareness and maturity (Kincaid 70). Thus, the mere knowledge of sex is sufficient to destroy the child's purity. The child is then constructed as an empty space, vulnerable to all exterior influences and immanently corruptible (Kincaid 7).

As a matter of course, those who wish to censor and edit the sexual content of American media legitimize their actions by citing the potential

91

degradation of children. This rhetoric has become so common and so widely accepted that most people refuse to interrogate its fundamental premise that the mere representation of sex, and in some cases only the mention of sex, will awaken children's sexual appetites and transform them into deviants.

Consider as an example the numerous controversies that have been associated with the Disney company in the past few years. The Boycott Disney Campaign began when a ten-year-old child who was viewing *The Lion King* noticed the word "sex" written in the clouds as Simba experiences the visitation of his father's ghost. This discovery unleashed a barrage of criticism that the Disney company was secretly trying to corrupt America's children. One of the more remarkable aspects of this public fury is that it failed to consider that millions of people (adults and children alike) viewed *The Lion King* without even noticing the offensive word. Thus, any presumed effort on the part of Disney to awaken the sexual appetites of children can only be construed as a resounding failure. Many cannot see the offending apparition even when they look for it. What is even more disturbing about this hysterical outburst of parental overprotectiveness is the implication that even the word "sex" might be a danger to children. The participants in the boycott were not objecting to the depiction of eroticism in a film that targets children, but to the virtually imperceptible representation of the term "sex" itself.

The Disney controversy reveals the tendency to perceive the corporation as an extension of the child's purity. Just as the child is often perceived as either entirely "free of any whiff of sexuality or ... somehow saturated in it" (Kincaid 183), the corporation must also eschew any suggestion of the sexual to be trusted with the entertainment of America's children. The association of any branch of the corporation with sex corrupts the entire body. When a Disney subsidiary released the film *Priest*, Elizabeth Dole initiated a sell-off of Disney stock by publicly suggesting that the company was tainted. Similar incidents include the effort to coerce Disney into denying homosexuals the right to congregate at its theme parks. One representative for this family-values campaign suggested that the company could remove all expressions of same-sex desire if it was also willing to ban all expressions of heterosexual affection, a recommendation that goes beyond mere homophobia by advancing the complete emptying of human sexuality from the park. The park then becomes the objective manifestation of the idealized inner life of the child, a space devoid of carnal knowledge and experience. The attempted purification of Disney also extends to objections over the corporation's decision to offer benefits to same-sex domestic partners.

One of the most disturbing aspects of this hyperbolic fear of children's sexual initiation is its extension to adolescents, a group that can be reasonably expected to have already begun experimenting with sex. There is a tendency within our culture to blind ourselves to the sexual potential of teenagers (Califia 39). Yet paradoxically, we must acknowledge that puberty is the beginning of sexual awareness and experimentation, and at least in the case of young males, it is the time when sexual drives are more powerful than they will be at any other period. Thus, the fight to prolong the sexual purity of the teenager is waged against biology. The protective parent can only hope that the child will forbear until he is married.

Perhaps the most revealing cultural manifestation of this paradoxical view of the adolescent lies in the controversies over condom distribution and sex education in schools. Many parents insist that such programs encourage adolescents to begin experimenting with sex. If the child is not given that option, she will remain ignorant of the possibility and will inadvertently abstain. The most potent argument against such willful blindness, of course, is the potential for AIDS infection that may result because teenagers could not, or would not, abstain. Parents' willingness to ignore the adversities that ensue when the sexually active are bereft of the necessary information to protect themselves must come from the personal assurance that the child without information and without permission will never engage in sexual activity. This position once again insists upon the protective emptiness of the child.

In its laws, our culture demands the sexual innocence of adolescence. The judicial repercussions against those unwise adults who have sex with an adolescent are severe and can involve lengthy prison terms. Legally, there is no consent on the part of the adolescent. Thus, all sex between adolescents and adults is rape. However, as a culture, we fail to interrogate the arbitrary nature of "age of consent laws, [which] do not take into consideration varying degrees of physical and emotional maturity" in teenagers (Califia 40). The law regards any sexual contact between an adult and an adolescent as fundamentally exploitative and, therefore, coercive (Kincaid 210). Of course, the need to prohibit and punish the sexual exploitation of children is a legitimate one, but is the erotic involvement between the adult and the teenager always exploitative? Is it manipulative even if the teenager is the aggressor? Must we assume then that the involvement between two adolescents is entirely free of power relations and potential coercion? After all, American society does not generally penalize sex between teenagers unless it involves rape. Does our legal apparatus on this issue then suggest that adolescents can only have sex if it is with someone equally inexperienced? If so, even our legal system prefers the sexual ignorance of children and is complicit in the program to maintain their emptiness. Yet at the age of 18, with little or no intermediary stage, the adolescent is (in the eyes of the law) suddenly transformed into a responsible adult with all of the knowledge necessary to be held fully accountable for her actions. This includes the knowledge about sexual propriety. Certainly, the 18-year-old man accused of rape is presumed from a legal standpoint to have sufficient information to know his actions are wrong.

The above cultural negotiations form the context for reading Rice's *Sleeping Beauty* novels, in which she subjects issues of consent and adolescent sexuality to constant interrogation, disputing those who insist upon the sexual ignorance of teenagers. Indeed, her *Beauty* series can be regarded as an extended metaphor that addresses the importance of sexual knowledge, both in theory and in practice, in the lives of adolescents. Beauty's erotic odyssey becomes a metaphorical representation of the volcanic passions of adolescence, and the consent of Beauty's parents to her exploitation suggests the necessity of enduring the inevitable sexual maturation of the child.

The eroticized child is a recurring character throughout Rice's canon. The child Mona in the novel *Lasher* seduces the adult Michael and is not in any way damaged by her experience. In fact, Mona is engaged in a deliberate effort to gain desired knowledge about sex, information that she cannot expect to acquire through normative relations with adults. She is the aggressor, and Michael's judgment is temporarily impaired so that his character need not endure the full responsibility and subsequent condemnation for his pedophilic actions. Similarly, in the novel *Belinda*, the titular character is a precocious teenager who becomes involved with an older man. Although the revelation of their involvement creates quite a scandal, there is little doubt that the young girl has benefited from the relationship. In both of these cases, the author interrogates the age of consent, suggesting that it does not fit with the reality of adolescent sexual drives. In both cases, Rice creates a character who is underage, yet is emotionally mature enough to manage a sexual relationship with an adult.

The *Beauty* novels offer a slightly altered perspective on children's sexuality, emphasizing the necessity of sex education, particularly through practice, if the adolescent is to understand and control her desires. Beauty is a 15-year-old girl who is awakened from 100 years of charmed sleep by the Prince. In her recounting of the Sleeping Beauty story, Rice accentuates the sexual implications that are latent in many fairy tales. The always unspoken eroticism that is implicit in stories where the princess is rescued by the prince and carried off to live happily ever after is exposed in a most explicit fashion. The unstated, yet inevitable consummation between the rescuer and the rescued is clearly portrayed. The subsequent deluge of sexual encounters that compose the narrative of the three novels is offered both as an exaggerated representation of the ferocious desires of adolescent sexuality and as a detailed, methodical conditioning and training of those desires. Beauty's rescue from her century of sleep is followed by forced servitude in Queen Eleanor's Castle, where Beauty is regarded as a royal sex slave and is subjected to a gauntlet of dehumanizing sexual activities, each designed to be more degrading than the last.

The Erotic Adventures of Sleeping Beauty includes three novels individually titled *The Claiming of Sleeping Beauty, Beauty's Punishment,* and *Beauty's Release.* Each novel includes a change of location for Beauty's servitude. She begins as a slave in the Prince's Castle. However, for an act of disobedience, she is sent to the Village where, no longer treated as a royal captive, she is harshly punished. After a period in the Village, she is abducted by a raiding party and carried off to the Sultan's Palace, from which she is eventually retrieved and returned to her parents. The pattern in the three novels involves a continuing degradation of the slave through increasingly dehumanizing punishments and sexual encounters. As a royal slave in the first novel, Beauty is the favorite of the Prince, who takes special interest in her training and punishment and who gluts his sexual longings at will. In the Prince's Castle, the punishments are ritualized, and the sexual encounters are usually limited to two people. After her transfer to the Village in the second novel, Beauty's punishments become more severe, and her sexual partners become more numerous. The punishments are more dehumanizing than those dispensed in the Castle. For instance, the slaves are forced to insert a phallus with a horse's tail protruding from the exposed end, suggesting the animal nature of their passion and servitude. In the Castle, a slave may be hung up in the Hall of Punishment or made to run the gauntlet of the Bridal Path, but the punishment is always controlled and artfully stylized, involving the undivided attention of nobility. In the Village, Beauty is carried in a wagon with other slaves, unceremoniously sold at auction, and subjected to a multitude of debased sexual partners. In the tavern, she becomes the erotic plaything of a whole troop of soldiers. However, the worst punishment in the Village is to be consigned to the pony stables to be sexually exploited by the stable boy. After her abduction by the Sultan's raiding party, Beauty and her companions are introduced to a still more debasing predicament. They are informed that they will be treated like beasts of burden and are instructed never to speak or to demonstrate the power of reason. The most obscene punishment at the Palace is to be banished to "corridors of miserable oblivion," where innumerable slaves are made to mimic statues, unmoving and unnoticed. This punishment signifies a complete loss of humanity: "Here we are nameless and nothing" (*Beauty's Release* 126). The Sultan's imperious disregard for the slaves' individual needs and identity is continued by the female genital mutilation within the Sultan's harem. The captives are also subject to the capriciousness of the Sultan's attentions. In the Castle, the slave enjoyed and maintained the prolonged attention of the monarch. Among the multitude of slaves at the Palace, the newly arrived Beauty cannot be certain that she will ever see the Sultan again after their first encounter. The bestial labors in the Village are literalized in the dehumanizing harem of the Sultan's Palace, where slaves are not even allowed to demonstrate the power of reason. The movement of the novels involves a decline in the stature of the protagonist from princess to peasant to beast.

The pattern of degradation that Rice employs in the *Beauty* novels reveals her preoccupation with the liberating qualities of sex, particularly of sadomasochistic sex. Here, Rice borrows from de Sade, whose work recognizes the anarchic potential of both pain and pleasure, their power to destroy certainty, and their tendency to subvert the standard morality (Morris 237). Sadomasochism is a fragmenting of the structures of the self, a dismantling and subsequent restructuring of identity. In this context, Beauty's sex education does not involve moralizing about the degradations and dangers of the sex act or about the perverse blending of pleasure and pain. Instead, her instruction emphasizes a reveling in the humiliations of the most degrading sex acts and punishments, a self-obliterating emersion in pleasure and torture, a complete erasure of pride and pretense: "Under the guise of force, the masters grant Beauty license to experience fully her most debased sexual desire" (Ramsland "Forced" 339). The slave Tristan observes the following:

> I was plunged into the depth of the Village, abandoned there. And it was luxurious suddenly, horribly luxurious, that so many should witness this delirium of abasement. If I must lose my pride, my will, my soul, let them revel in it [*Beauty's Punishment* 105].

Paradoxically, the self-liberation and immolation is achieved through an increasing application of discipline and order, through a surrendering to the will of another. Thus, the freedom that is achieved is a freedom from vanities and moralities. It is a resignation to humiliation and abuse. A master "[enables] them to explore capacities for pleasure and surrender which they might resist on their own" (Ramsland "Forced" 323). The slaves emerge from their servitude with "wisdom, patience, and self-discipline," with a full understanding and acceptance of their deepest desires, and with an appreciation for the mutual suffering of humanity (Ramsland *Prism* 216).

The implicit views on sexual socialization in Rice's *Beauty* series defy the conventional wisdom and morality, to say the least. It is hardly thinkable that the contemporary parent would willingly subject her child to such degradation. Yet in the context of the novels, parents voluntarily submit their children to the rigors of the Castle so that those children can learn self-discipline. When the Prince rescues Beauty and her parents, he demands her as a reward and tribute. He persuades her parents to comply by reminding them of their own valuable servitude in the Castle. Although saddened by the loss of their daughter, Beauty's parents are assured that her bondage will not last forever and that she will be returned "greatly enhanced in wisdom and beauty" (*Claiming* 16). Leon, another occupant of Queen Eleanor's domain, explains the benefits of service to the Castle:

> They are returned to their kingdoms when the Queen so wishes, and obviously very much better off for their service here. They're not so vain any longer; they have great self-control and often a different view of the world, one which enables them to achieve great understanding [*Claiming* 90].

The Prince later defines the understanding that is born out of bondage: "I realized then that there would be endless variations in humiliation. It was not a hierarchy of punishments I faced; it was rather endless changes" (*Claiming* 208). The Prince's newly attained wisdom resembles the wisdom that one must demonstrate strength in the face of life's inevitable adversities and humiliations. The parents of the Castle slaves can expect their children to emerge from their servitude with an enhanced capacity to brook life's toils and troubles. The servitude is a lengthy lesson in bearing up under hardship.

Rice interrogates the paradoxical practice of American parents who shield their children from the knowledge that would permit their children to cope more effectively with the inevitable, frequent tribulations of life. The slaves of the Castle and the subsequent venues directly confront those experiences that our culture defines as irredeemably degrading and destructive, particularly to the young. These practices are commonly constructed as the introduction to a life of corruption and debauchery. Yet contrary to popular wisdom about the early sexualizing of children, the characters remain innocent despite the bestial degradations of their servitude. Through this unique perspective, Rice expresses her belief that "the erotic and the wholesome are not mutually exclusive" (Riley 63). "She write[s] about people who ... [can] submit to extreme degradation, yet retain their integrity and dignity" (Ramsland "Forced" 338).

The characters of the *Beauty* novels emerge from their captivity remarkably unscathed, particularly when one considers that the rigors of their enslavement would kill the average individual. It is difficult to imagine that Beauty could be raped by an entire troop of soldiers and experience no detrimental physical effects, not even pregnancy. Yet she returns to her parents at the end of the third novel and has only wisdom and confidence to show for her experiences. This account of sexual torture is a burlesque of the tendency within our culture to view sex as dirty and degrading, the very bias that motivates parents to shield their children from sexual knowledge and experience. The characters within the novels demonstrate an equally exaggerated, yet antithetical indifference toward the corruptions of the flesh. Through the hyperbolic lampooning of this deep-rooted fear, Rice reveals her conviction that "sex is good," not vile (Roberts *Rice* 141), that adolescents benefit from sexual knowledge, and that the only degrading aspect of the erotic is the belief that sex is dirty.

Rice recuperates even those aspects of sex that are regarded in our culture as the most threatening to the young. In the collection of interviews compiled by Michael Riley, Rice proudly announces that she took her son to see the Gay Pride Parade in San Francisco because she wanted him to have that unique experience before the family left California. It is this type of experience from which many or most American parents would seek to shield their children, justifying their concern by citing the fear that exposure to such knowledge would encourage emulation. Rice's practice of exposing her son to sexual diversity is consistent with the parenting in the *Beauty* novels. The King and Queen recognize that Beauty will grow through carnal knowledge, even if that knowledge might be socially constructed as deviant. Beauty's pleasurable lesbian experiences in the Sultan's Palace do not interfere with her desire for men; they merely broaden the scope of her longings.

One of the more commonly cited justifications for criminalizing sex between adults and adolescents is the power differential that exists between the generations. The greater knowledge and enhanced influence of the adult creates the potential for the exploitation of the younger party. Rice cross-examines this cultural assumption by emphasizing the imbalance of power that exists between the practitioners of S & M. In the *Beauty* novels, the asymmetrical distribution of authority and influence between masters and slaves constitutes a burlesque of our cultural bias against such arrangements. Indeed, the power imbalance specifically results in coercion, abuse, and exploitation, but the misused individuals are not harmed by their mistreatment. In fact, they are improved:

> It is the Master who creates the order, the Master who lifts that slave out of the engulfing chaos of abuse, and disciplines the slave, refines him.... Over and over we are lost ... only to be retrieved by the Master [*Beauty's Punishment* 178–79].

Rice suggests that the relationship between unequal partners is instructive. Thus she invokes the Greek pederastic tradition in which the intergenerational bond involves a pedagogical element (Greenberg 148). The slave Tristan remarks that his master "guide[s]" him "to greater and greater revelations" (*Beauty's Punishment* 208).

Rice recuperates the potential coerciveness of the pederastic match, not by suggesting that the youth is unaffected by the manipulations of the more powerful partner, but by suggesting that the youth becomes saturated with, and altered by, that power. The adolescent does not escape the transformative power of exploitation and abuse, but it improves him. The master both inflicts the pain and teaches the slave how to endure it. The tolerance for punishment and the control of passion emphasized by the master teaches the slaves to cope with the painful vicissitudes of their lives as future rulers. Since the slaves in the Castle are princes and princesses, the rigorous exposure to the coercive will of others demonstrates by example how to dominate and rule. When both Beauty and Laurent are released from their bondage, they immediately demonstrate their newly attained skills in governance. Beauty dominates the suitor of her arranged marriage so thoroughly that he decides to forgo the match and submit to training in Queen Eleanor's Castle. Upon the ascension to his father's vacated throne, Laurent assumes the seat of government quite easily:

> None of this was difficult, really, yet I knew that many a European Kingdom fell because a new monarch could not do it. And I saw the look of relief on the faces of my subjects when they realized that their young King exercised authority easily and naturally, that he directed all matters of government, both large and small, with great personal attention and force [*Beauty's Release* 232].

Rather than insisting upon the adolescent's protective ignorance of sex, Rice insists that knowledge of the erotic, gained through a match between the experienced and the inexperienced, is the most effective means of attaining control over oneself and one's environment.

It is difficult to identify a topic that is more subversive of American family values than the sexual initiation of minors by adults, yet Rice consistently broaches the topic. However, her representation of this inflammatory subject is not unmitigated by portrayals of normative romantic relations. As with most of the controversial issues that she addresses, Rice's radicalism is tempered by an insistence upon the traditional marital bond that emerges from even the most eccentric, debauched beginnings. As an advocate of promiscuous and guiltless sex, she has a curious tendency to assume that all relations will end in a traditional match between consenting adults. Indeed, the intemperate libidinal indulgences common to the inhabitants of the Castle, Village, and Palace encourage the slaves to seek meaningful, forbidden relations with single partners. The culmination of Beauty's passions in the Castle results when she meets Prince Alexi in secret; they share their personal experiences and consummate their desire for each other. Beauty develops a similar bond with Tristan in the Village and with Laurent in the Palace. Indeed, the *Beauty* series ends with the aristocratic marriage of Beauty and Laurent and a presumption of monogamy and fidelity. Evidently, Rice can only conceive of promiscuity and polymorphous sexual longings as a preparation for an exalted, lengthy monogamous bond between members of the opposite sex. All of the debauchery is merely instrumental in the creation of a stronger bond. Thus, Beauty's sex education is not so subversive after all. The techniques may be unconventional, but the objective is quite traditional.

The conclusion of the series is very conventional in yet another way. It legitimizes and maintains the patriarchal power structure that is so prevalent in fairy tales and pornography. Rice defies orthodox gender construction by allowing her female characters to possess a sexual appetite that is equally voracious to that of men, and she does not suggest that they are any less desirable for their experience. Yet she does, nevertheless, maintain and emphasize the traditional gender-power asymmetry that is common in conventional narratives. Beauty may enjoy sex with many people, including women, but the objective of her longings remains domination by a man. Upon the return of Beauty to her father's castle, she demonstrates an uncharacteristic willfulness for a female in a romance narrative by refusing all suitors. However, when King Laurent comes to claim her, she becomes the soul of compliance to the male will. Laurent makes it clear that he will dominate her and that she will be his sex slave. Moreover, the narrative implies that this is just what Beauty has been waiting for, a man sufficiently knowledgeable about domination to circumvent her will. Laurent imposes his desires with confidence and authority: "You will marry me, Princess. You will be my Queen and my slave." And Beauty reveals her longing for his mastery: "O, Laurent, I never dared dream of this moment" (*Beauty's Release* 235). Such a conclusion can hardly be construed as progressive even if the woman is complicit and equally experienced in sexual matters.

There are a number of potential explanations for Rice's decision to temper her radicalism with some very conventional conclusions. Not the least among these explanations is the desire to remain consistent with the fairy tale, which necessitates that protagonists live together "happily ever after." If the *Beauty* novels are to be regarded as a literalization of the latent eroticism in fairy tales and other children's literature, then it is important that she maintain an ostensible compliance with the narrative protocol of that genre to make her point. The assertion that the prince and princess will live "a good deal happier ... than anyone could ever guess" (*Beauty's Release* 238) conforms with the expected final line of the fairy tale at the same time that it highlights the erotic nature of the protagonists' happiness. Beauty and Laurent can be expected to live very happily because they are so skilled in pleasing each other sexually. The final line preserves the ostensible innocence and integrity of the fairy tale while suggesting that childhood is saturated with sexual longings and that both success in marriage and happiness as adults relies upon prior carnal knowledge.

The conventional conclusion also emphasizes Rice's central point about sex education. The early introduction of adolescents to sexual experience, even with adults, does not necessarily disrupt the youngster's normative sexual development. It does not nullify the child's desire for a family, and it does not always result in psychopathology. Sometimes those individuals who experience early carnal knowledge are happier and better adjusted than those who abstained until marriage. The protagonists of the *Beauty* novels are not only happy in their marriage, but much happier "than anyone could ever guess."

In the context of American cultural negotiations over the inevitable sex education and initiation of children and adolescents, Rice's *Beauty* novels offer a unique perspective. She boldly challenges our tendency to transform all discussions of children's sexual genesis into a "melodrama of monsters and innocents" (Kincaid 27). The most fundamental assumption that she supplants is the often uninterrogated belief that sex is corruptive and dirty. Rice believes that the route to wisdom is through knowledge of the flesh (Riley 20) and that the individual can be both sexually experienced and innocent. However, as in much of her work, she synthesizes heretical assumptions about sex with orthodox objectives as if sexual experimentation were merely a prelude to a conventional marriage and traditional gender-power relations.

Chapter 5

EXIT TO EDEN:
THE BODY, THE SPECTACLE,
AND THE TRANSGRESSIVE SPACE

In her biography, Anne Rice praises the successes of *Exit to Eden* (1985): "I think getting *Exit to Eden* published in hardcover is one of the most daring things that happened.... We published that between hardcovers in America! What an accomplishment!" (Ramsland *Prism* 235) The author's astonishment and enthusiasm over what would seem to be a minimal accomplishment for a popular writer implies that the issuing of the novel in a respectable form was a breach of conventional literary standards and publication etiquette. The novel is a transgression. The wild sadomasochistic fantasies that subvert the conventions of literary decency are arrested or "contained" within the licensed space of the hardcover. Transgression has been endorsed but enclosed and controlled by the confinement of the publishing industry's respectable cover. The author describes the novel as "a heightened form of porn" (Ramsland *Prism* 228). Thus, her triumph involves the elevation of that which has been constituted as low culture. It dignifies base subject matter.

Exit to Eden is narrated and structured by the alternating voices of Lisa Kelly and Elliot Slater. The former is the creator and manager of The Club, an island paradise for advocates of sadomasochism. It is a space where members are permitted to act out their most repressed sexual fantasies in an environment of openness and acceptance. Elliot is a volunteer slave on the island, a person who has agreed to be sexually used by the rich, wealthy club members for a period of two years. The narrative is an unconventional love story about Lisa and Elliot overcoming the restrictions of The Club to nurture the affections of the traditional bourgeois marriage.

The novel borrows heavily from the popular carnival tradition of the Middle Ages. Because Rice is a native of New Orleans, we can assume that she is intimately acquainted with the carnivalesque. It may even be said that she employs the carnival to its own destruction. She pays homage, maintains a respectable facade, and undermines long-standing literary norms simultaneously.

Mikhail Bakhtin details the recurring features of the medieval celebrations in his landmark study *Rabelais and His World*. He describes the period of unrestrained riot in which the common people have their will. He cites the mock rituals, involving the crowning and uncrowning of comic and legitimate authority, and the whippings and abusive language leveled at rascals and aristocrats alike. He describes the carnival as a place in which the normative standards of the society are ridiculed and the traditional social hierarchy is inverted. He emphasizes the spectacle of the grotesque body that is paraded down the street, an emblem of the chaotic festival atmosphere. For a brief period, democracy and free speech prevail. However, at the conclusion of the celebration, the legitimate powers reassert their authority, and order is restored.

Much scholarship in recent years has sought to trace the impact of the carnival tradition on literary texts, particularly on works of the Early Modern period. However, more infrequent are studies delineating the carnival attributes of contemporary popular culture, even though the medieval carnival was a production and celebration of the common people. In this chapter, I endeavor to reveal the author's unconventional appropriation of the carnival tradition and to demonstrate its topical application to *Exit to Eden* and contemporary popular culture.

Bakhtin described the carnival as a "second life of the people, who for a time entered the utopian realm of community, freedom, equality, and abundance." It is a "temporary liberation from the prevailing truth and from the established order" (Bahktin 9–10). This description, except for a few meaningful alterations, accurately represents the environment and objective of The Club. The riotous release of the holiday atmosphere, however, assumes a more specific form at Rice's Caribbean resort. The participants enjoy a complete release of libidinal fantasies. Lisa describes the staff as "geniuses of exotic sex" (165). Their purpose is to facilitate every whim of members who have paid as much as $250,000 for the right to enjoy the facility's freedoms. The staff has contrived countless sexual games for the members' enjoyment. These include activities such as wrestling matches in which the loser becomes the passive object of the winner's sexual aggression, carnival games in which naked slaves are the objects of numerous humiliations, and public spectacles in which volunteer slaves are paraded around the island and displayed on an auction block. Of course, these activities do not include the myriad of pleasures that the members can invent in the privacy of their own suite with the aid of a submissive, yet eager slave.

Rice, however, makes an important alteration in the carnival's release of pent-up energies. Although The Club is a place where erotic dreams can be realized with wanton abandon, it is nevertheless highly systematized. The many strict rules and regulations create an economy of licensed pleasures. The Club's director insists that this "kind of sex has its rituals, its limits, and its rules" (109). The slave is required to obey the commands of members and trainers, or she is publicly pilloried. Yet even punishments are managed. Upon arriving at the island, slaves are assured that whippings will never be so severe as to break the skin or leave permanent scars. The objective of the punishments seems to be fear and humiliation rather than intense physical pain. Even the trainers are subject to specific guidelines. When Lisa, the founder of The Club escapes with Elliot from the island, she violates the system's most fundamental rule, which prohibits breaking the slave's contract or allowing her personal passions to interfere with the execution of her duties. Moreover, the elaborate rituals involved in the trade of slaves on the island are further signs of control. Paradoxically, the regulations facilitate rather than undermine holiday release.

For the advocates of sadomasochistic pleasures, rules and systems are desirable. To submit to another's control or to exercise dominance over a submissive partner constitutes the realization of their libidinal dreams. To face punishment for the breach of island rituals facilitates the release of the participant's deep fantasies. Thus order and structure is an integral aspect of release.

Only in the representation of The Club's members is the riotous atmosphere of the popular festivals carefully observed. Bakhtin notes that the carnival emphasizes the members' universality over their singularity; everyone participates (7). The members of The Club are similarly represented in throngs. They are seen eating, drinking, dancing, gambling, and copulating as a mass. The imagery associated with the island's "sports arcade" creates the claustrophobic atmosphere of the popular celebration. The streets are choked with people:

> Guests moved in and out of the buildings. And hundreds strolled on the white sand, shirts open to the waist, drinks in hand. ... The crowd thickened around us. I felt claustrophobic as pant legs and boots and coats brushed against me [132–33].

The 3,000 guests who have arrived for the beginning of the new season are packed so tightly that they breach the social etiquette that designates personal space, the private, transgressive space where bodies meet only in passion. The author compares her scene to Hieronymus Bosch's *Garden of Earthly Delights*, in which writhing bodies are depicted in multiple convolutions. Of course, paradise, sensuality, and torture are the major themes of that painter's triptych.

In carnivalesque literature, the revelers are composed of members of the lower classes, gathered together for the overthrow of hierarchical conventions and for a period of freedom from the restrictions of class. The popular festivities were antithetical to those of high society, whose gatherings were characterized by ritual, order, and decorum. In this latter tradition, the aristocratic body is displayed as solitary, while the peasant body is collective. In *Exit to Eden*, the convention has been inverted. The creators of The Club have made a purposeful effort to fashion the resort as an exclusive environment for the rich. The price of admission for one year lies outside the reach of all but the most wealthy. Moreover, the only people permitted to act with carnivalesque freedom are those wealthy members. Thus, in the novel, the aristocratic class is presented as an indistinct mass seeking to glut its base appetites, while the slaves are objects of an individual scrutiny that emphasizes every feature of their singular anatomies. The popular festival becomes restricted and private.

The most distinctive feature of holiday release is inversion. The world is turned "topsy turvy" (Greenblatt 66). Power structures are mocked and parodied. Codes of decency are overturned. The low are elevated above the privileged. The grotesque is admired. Confusion replaces good order and propriety. Rice applies carnival inversion to contemporary social structures, which are characterized, at least nominally, by democracy. The holiday reversal constitutes a restoration of an obsolete order, the aristocratic social structure that values one class above another and institutes slavery and human degradation. In the novel, the festival includes the right to practice a now-repugnant value system, and to live in a fashion that Western culture has deemed unacceptable. Of course, the representation of class structure has additional implications within the novel, and these will be taken up later in the chapter.

The holiday inversions include representations of the human body. The carnival shifts the cultural privilege of the "high, spiritual, ideal, and abstract" in the hierarchy of the body to an emphasis on its material functioning. Eating, drinking, defecating, and copulating are elevated above mind and spirit (Bakhtin 18–19). Rabelais' world is a visceral, carnal world. The moral descent is also a spatial descent. The movement downward from head and heart to stomach, genitals, and buttocks parallels the decline of normative standards of decency. Western philosophy has traditionally emphasized the superiority of the soul and mind over the body, which was constituted as the devil's playground. In the Middle Ages, the church urged the negation of the body, which was the center of temptation and transgression; life was a lengthy preparation for death. The low functions of the body were politicized and associated with the devil and hell. Only the mind and soul could transcend gross flesh to achieve mystical union with divinity. The Christian soul needed to overcome bodily limitations and enticements to attain salvation. The carnival, with its celebration of the grotesque body and its scatological functions, constituted the temporary release and overturning of ideological and cultural assumptions regarding corporeality. The politics of the body was inverted. Grotesque functions were a component of the life cycle, facilitating the procreative process and the vicissitudes of human development, and were elevated above the spiritual.

Certainly, The Club conforms to the festival's inversion of body politics. There is no effort among either staff or members to achieve any mystical union of amorous souls. Only the life of the body is indulged. The rules of The Club are designed to minimize the possibility of intimacy. The slaves are not generally the property of any individual, so promiscuity and variety are the norms. The slaves are handed from trainer to trainer and guest to guest. The class structure that predominates on the island negates the possibility that a bond of equal opposites, forming the normative sexual union, will occur. When Lisa and Elliot begin to experience deep sentiments for each other, sentiments that necessitate the indulgence of mind and body, they must escape from the island to realize their conventional fantasy. Lisa recognizes that The Club's rituals have been "protecting" her from emotional involvement (288). Here, we begin to see that the fantasy island is limited in the dreams that it can facilitate. There is no place for common romance. Only carnal indulgence is given free reign.

The body politics of the novel have an additional dimension, one that overturns carnival inversion, creating a meaningful break with tradition. As previously stated, the grotesque body reigned as the symbolic figuration of the festival environment. On the grotesque form, bulges and orifices, rather that smoothness and finish, are accentuated. The carnival body threatens to break all bounds of decency. It promises to fracture structure and limitation, signifying the riotous release of the body politic at the height of the carnival season and threatening to transgress the bounds of decency and civility (Bakhtin 316–18). Just as the grotesque body refuses to obey the conventions of the classical human form, the image of human beauty, the festival refuses to honor the limitations that the power structure imposes upon the populace. The carnival form is the image of chaos, and the holiday is the realization of its revolutionary program.

Traditionally, the bulging carnival body is contrasted to the form of classical statuary that emphasizes the beauty and finish of the human form. It possesses "no openings or orifices" (Stallybrass and White 22). The classical form is generally raised on a pedestal and fully illuminated so that the observer must "gaze up at the figure and wonder." Its elevation reveals once again the spatializing of morality and the literalization of the nominal value distinction between high and low. The spectator is conditioned by presentation to regard the figure on the pedestal with admiration, to accept it as the image of high culture. The orderly nature of the classical body itself parallels the highly structured society. The classical form politely observes the conventions of human beauty. It does not threaten to break the bonds of the flesh. It is not the emblem of chaos and becoming, but of order, restraint, and temperance. It signifies the values of the elite power structure (Stallybrass and White 21–22).

Rice takes some liberties with the distinction between the grotesque and the classical. The Club could be regarded, paradoxically, as an aristocracy of the beautiful. However, the classical beauty on the island is found among the slave and trainer population, not among the members, who must be regarded as the world's monied elite. The goal of the resort is to create a carnal paradise of uninterrupted sexual arousal and fulfillment. This is actualized only by the spectacle of the classical body. The newly arrived, unclothed slaves are paraded around the island for the pleasure of all involved. They eventually end up on the auction block, a well-lit pedestal upon which they can be viewed. The spectacle creates a social paradox, altering the carnival tradition. While those individuals made to walk the auction runway are slaves who are contracted to be constantly humiliated and sexually manipulated for a two-year period, they are nevertheless the objects of wonder, admiration, and desire among their social superiors. The slave is elevated spatially as she marches down the runway and politically as she becomes a spectacle for the gaze of the lascivious membership. The slave is marginal and central. While she is socially the lowest participant at the resort, symbolically she is irreplaceable. Without her physical impressiveness, The Club's project would be impossible. The function of the resort rests entirely upon the broad, well-shaped shoulders of the submissive slaves. The oppositions of praise and humiliation and of master and slave are deconstructed within the isolated island society. The slave is simultaneously high and low, raised and repressed, or perhaps more accurately, raised as she is repressed.

Whereas the grotesque body is the appropriate symbol for the rampage of the popular holiday, the classical form is the fitting representation of The Club's political structure. The isolated society is characterized by form, union, and plan. It is the paragon of order and system. Thus, it is aptly signified by the smooth finish of the perfected human frame. The operations of this highly structured government parallel the classical body, on which all bulges and orifices are minimized. The closure of all bodily openings suggests the isolation of the island paradise, which is accessible to only a select few. Any action that disrupts the fluid movements of The Club's management is subject to behavioral modification. Discipline is the technology for producing docile bodies, social subjects who do not disrupt the political structure (Foucault *Discipline* 136). The emphasis on the well-developed musculature of the slave body suggests the combination of sensuality, beauty, power, strength, and torture that is fundamental to the resort's operation.

Another telling difference between the classical form and the fleshy spectacle of the auction runway is the presence of the slave's sexualized body. This body does not represent abstraction or aesthetic contemplation of the spiritual beauty of humanity for the neutered gaze of cultured admirers. It signifies sex and is intended to inspire base lust. The alteration in the tradition of the classical body is represented by one grotesque attribute: the aroused phallus that, Elliot observes, is a feature of every male slave. Signifying desire and the disruption of order, the protruding phallus breaks the smoothness and finish of the classical body. However, it also suggests strictly controlled lust that finds its outlet only when the trainer or member permits it.

The whipping post, at which the disobedient slaves are pilloried by their trainers, constitutes yet another site of inversion, of social and sexual paradox. In the novel, Lisa brings Elliot to the platform to be whipped for some inconsequential infraction of club etiquette. Lisa observes that her slave does not "like the idea of being shackled, whipped in front of spectators" (143), and she can tell that the event has both aroused and frightened him. She further remarks that she has come to "loath" the sheer artifice of the public flagellations (147). The beatings are theatrical, intended to please a crowd of onlookers as well as the participants. In the carnival activities, physical abuse was part of the symbolic uncrowning of authority. A figure, often a mock king, was beaten to represent the deposing of the contemporary power structure and the replacing of that apparatus with the popular voice of the people. Although the event was only figural, it was staged for the festival crowd and was to signify both the holiday release of restraints and the flagellation of authority (Bakhtin 197–99). On The Club's platform, the beating is both literal and symbolic, intended to facilitate arousal and thus the release of sexual restraints. The thrashing of the festival king of the medieval carnival constituted an uncrowning and mocking of legitimate authority. Perhaps the flagellation of the slaves suggests the repudiation of social and sexual pretensions, the most fundamental objective of the resort.

The punishment is a theatrical moment that is intended to reinforce the shared values and desires of guests and slaves alike. In his groundbreaking work *Discipline and Punish*, Michel Foucault addresses the spectacle of power in which the transgressor's crimes are actually inscribed upon his body as a manifestation and validation of the king's authority. Transgression of the laws was regarded as an injury against the monarch herself, and the public display of torture, which Foucault named the "carnival of atrocity," reconstitutes and consolidates the sovereign's authority. Trespasses against monarchical control actually served the interests of the power apparatus because it offered an opportunity to make a dramatic display of its invulnerability (32–69).

At the whipping post, Elliot's body becomes the site of a reaffirmation of communal values, emphasizing the sadomasochistic fantasies of all the participants at The Club. The usual prioritizing of pleasure above pain is deconstructed at the post. Pain is pleasure; the distinction collapses in the S & M paradise. Despite his initial reluctance, Elliot himself is the most willing participant within the spectacle. He signed on at the resort to get caught up in the pain, pleasure, and humiliation, to experience a "harrowing of the soul" (32). In the "carnival of atrocity," the transgressor's actions threaten the values of the state. Thus, he must be publicly purged for the maintenance of order. At The Club, the trespass is central. Although it is constructed as a threat to the system, it is actually vital to maintaining that system. There can be no S & M fantasy without torture. So transgression upholds the fundamental necessities of the communal environment by manufacturing a pretext for abuse. The onlookers receive what they have paid for when the slave is punished, and the slave receives the stimulation for which he contracted with the organization.

The practice of inscribing the sin of the transgressor upon his flesh is also part of The Club's technology of pain and humiliation. After Elliot inappropriately woos the crowd on the runway of the auction block, attendants record the infraction upon his flesh with a grease pen. Here again, sin is recuperated within the sexual economy of the resort. Elliot becomes a walking billboard for club management, wearing their signature, "Proud

Slave." His degradation becomes a symbol of the wages of transgression and helps to invigorate the values of club participants. They have come to the resort to shame or be shamed. Thus, the dishonored slave reinforces their desires and reaffirms their reasons for enrolling. The membership is obviously what sustains The Club, so Elliot's trespass is ultimately instrumental in the maintenance of the power that degrades him.

If the slave desires degradation and punishment, then those eventualities offer no threat. Indeed, at The Club, the slave has the power, determining the occasion and the extent of the penalty. There is a reversal of the master-slave relationship (Ramsland *Prism* 230). Often, the master actually serves the slave's will. On several occasions, Lisa observes that the punishments constitute a fulfillment of the servant's contract. The slave has a legal agreement that guarantees her torture. Thus, The Club is offering a service in a capitalist economy of sex. One of the principal consumers is the slave who, paradoxically, is paid to consume those services. The slave is also in a position to discontinue the punishment at will by terminating her contract. Here, the distinctions between power and vulnerability, between resistance and surrender, collapse (Ramsland *Prism* 230–31).

In the carnival, the flagellation of the festival king symbolizes the death and regeneration of the year, and much of the grotesque imagery is intended to emphasize this duality. The natural, vulgar processes of the human body are symbolic deaths, but they are also part of the regenerative process (Bakhtin 197). Rice suggests that this same duality is an integral aspect of S & M fantasies. In a conversation with his father, Elliot cites the Freudian duality between eros and thanatos, the union of the sex and death drives (196). Similarly, the punishments of The Club are symbolic executions that are intended to result in sexual arousal. The beatings inspire the fear of death in their subjects, and this fear assures the sexual performance both of those same subjects and of members who are stimulated by the spectacle of power. Thus, death and sex are inexorably linked. In a broader sense, that which threatens to obliterate humanity also guarantees its perpetuation.

This theme is related to the seasonal cycle that includes the annual birth and demise of nature, the guarantee that death will arrive again after life in the spring. Of course, the carnival has been associated with seasonal alterations for thousands of years. The cultures of the ancient world celebrated this cycle of life in their fertility rites, and Anne Rice refers to many of these festivals in this and in other novels, particularly in the *Vampire Chronicles*. *Exit to Eden* is structured upon the cycle. The beginning of the novel includes the arrival of members and staff for the start of the "new season." The resort's functioning is dictated by the alteration in nature. The elemental structure of the novel moves through a love affair between Lisa and Elliot, an escape from the institutional sterility of the resort, a symbolic separation that signifies the temporary demise of love, and the eventual and permanent reunion that promises marriage and, implicitly, new life for both the lovers and their offspring. The Club itself is associated with fertility. It is a site of continual sexual fulfillment. Lisa refers to the resort as a "great womb." There is also the figural implication of a resort called Eden. In this context, movements within the novel become scriptural allusions to humanity's origins in the garden and its eventual expulsion from the same. However, the death of innocence led eventually to life. Of course, these allusions that are associated with the resort are ironic because it is difficult for the average person to reconcile the idea of Edenic innocence with sadomasochism. Probably, the author wishes to equate the integrity of those who know what they want sexually with the openness and simplicity of the scriptural paradise, suggesting that guilty pleasure need not be an inevitable outcome of sexual abandonment.

The mockery of authority that is an integral part of carnival inversion extends to the society's most sacred institution: the official religion (Greenblatt 65). The atmosphere of Rice's novel is no exception to that tradition. Indeed, the author has structured the novel upon the basic contrast between the exterior world, which is characterized by the oppressive sexual morality of religions that demand uniformity of desire among the diversity of humanity, and the sexually liberated "womb" of The Club. Of course, consistent with her own preoccupations, the author aims her satiric barbs specifically at the Catholic Church, with which she seems to maintain a love-hate relationship. Much of the parody of church morality is achieved through the inversion of religious symbolism within the context of the island (Ramsland *Prism* 226). One of the most striking appropriations of church ritual is symbolically present in the very act of sadomasochistic sex: the chastising of the sinful flesh. The implications of this parallel are broad. Those fixated on the link between pleasure and pain are acting out a subconscious guilt that is generated by constant exposure to religious dogma. Thus, the thrashing of the masochist is the punishment for lust.

Some of the specific references to Catholicism reinforce the above reading. The three chief trainers at The Club (Lisa, Richard, and Scott), the individuals responsible for initiating punishment, are referred to as the "holy trinity" (61–62). Moreover, at the whipping post, Elliot kisses the trainer's strap in the pose of religious devotion:

> I kissed it the way Catholics kiss the crucifix on display in the
> church on Good Friday, and the warmth spread all through me
> at the feel of the leather against my lips [67].

The allusions to crucifixion and Good Friday reinforce the notion of torture as a form of religious devotion. Elliot becomes the mock image of the dying messiah who accepts his suffering in a theatrical gesture of selflessness that is intended to purge the collective. Elliot's assertion that he hopes to experience a "harrowing of the soul" at The Club takes on a new meaning in the carnival's religious context. Indeed, as will be discussed later, Elliot has his own personal demons to work out at the resort, specifically his fear of death. Elliot believes that The Club will be his "salvation" and perhaps even the "salvation" of the world (222–24). The expression, "harrowing of the soul," implies a cleansing through pain and suffering. In the same conversation, Elliot enigmatically appropriates scripture, calling his desire to spend two years in Eden "the word made flesh" (32). He associates this phrase with the unadulterated pursuit of pleasure, the desire to touch his sexual heart of darkness: "the dark and heated world that exists behind the civilized face in the mirror" (32). The phrase "word made flesh," alluding to Christ, exploits once again the paradox that ultimate fulfillment can be achieved through suffering and death.

There are additional allusions to religion, ones that specifically indict the prevailing sexual norms. Lisa's family is so strictly religious that she is unwilling to tell them of her occupation, fearing their condemnation. Her father accepts the sexual doctrines of the Church without question: chastity is superior to an active sex life because sex is "filthy," and homosexual impulses should be repressed (193). It is easy to see how Lisa would rebel against such a rigorous doctrine, and her life at The Club can be perceived as just that rebellion because she practices unrestrained sex with both men and women. Elliot's family is not religious, but nevertheless, it harbors a restrictive view of sexuality. Elliot's father is an atheist who is sexually liberated, but he believes that S & M is pathological (195). He threatens to have Elliot committed when he hears of his son's plans to enter servitude.

Rice does not fail to address the issue of gender inequities. In the carnival, the woman's womb is recognized as the source of fertility, the quality most honored by the festival season. Although the tradition maintains the restrictive notion that involvement with a woman is degrading, the degradation is for the purposes of procreation (Bakhtin 240). Such a notion cannot be regarded as progressive or gender conscious, but it is a step above the outright condemnation of women's sexuality that is a part of church dogma. Of course, *Exit to Eden* includes a much more progressive notion of gender equality. Lisa is the figural representation of this view. Her behavior undermines sexual stereotypes. Western society has constructed women as the passive gender for whom, in the past, the mere mention of sex was a breach of honor. Yet Lisa plainly subverts this social conditioning. She is not just a participant in the debauchery at the island resort, she is the principal instigator, the person who conceived many of the kinky games that are intended to stimulate the guests. Moreover, in the language of S & M, she is a dominatrix, exercising her power over males, subduing them, and making them obey her will. Her position inverts gender hierarchy in the public space of the resort and in the privacy of her bedroom, where she is the sexual aggressor. She undermines gender categories through her choice of partners as well. Before the arrival of Elliot, she almost exclusively chooses women for attendant slaves. Thus, she disregards cultural prohibitions against homoerotic activity, one of the principal topics that the Church exploits to consolidate its power over the sexual morality of the populace. Elliot also engages in alternative sexual practices before and after his arrival at the resort. While still in San Francisco, he maintains that his only interest is in men, whom he regards as the "exotic sex." However, his experiences with Lisa alter this predisposition. Both of these characters are coded as "sexual outlaws" who must eventually reform.

Still another paradox of The Club emerges from the theatrical motif in the novel. Eden is a place where the individual is permitted to act out her buried sexual fantasies to achieve the ecstasy of erotic fulfillment. The operative word is "act." These fantasies can only be achieved through roleplaying. Yet they are an expression of the individual's most intimate self, the one that she hides from the world. Thus, the opposition between fantasy and reality disintegrates within the context of The Club. The fantasy that is generally associated with unreality becomes a literalization of personal truth. Paradoxically, the role of the obedient social and sexual subject that the individual plays for the world may be the real theater piece. The roles played at the club are at least a portion of the real self. After her separation from Elliot in New Orleans, Lisa contacts her friend Martin for counsel. He reminds her that the relationship she has with Elliot was begotten in complete sexual openness, in an environment of honesty. Moreover, she comes to identify with a transvestite in a bar on Bourbon Street. Ostensibly, Lisa appreciates the entertainer because she is a "sexual outlaw" who does not care what other people think, but an additional implication is associated with the idea of masquerade. The presence of a transvestite raises a compelling philosophical question: which is more real, the interior or the exterior self? Is the transvestite a woman trapped in a man's body or simply a man impersonating a woman? These questions lie at the heart of Lisa's dilemma as she interrogates her involvement with The Club and Elliot. Which is preferable, the performance on the island in which she, like the drag queen, subverts gender categories to actualize some inner compulsion, or the masquerade of sexual uniformity that institutions impose upon the social subject?

Although Rice finally endorses a very conventional notion of sexual fulfillment, one whose politics will be analyzed later, she first interrogates America's hypocritical attitude toward sexuality. She exposes what theorist Alan Sinfield has termed an ideological "faultline" (Sinfield *Faultlines* 9), a paradox created by the juxtaposition of two competing ideological positions within a given discourse or social context. Elliot is a photojournalist whose experiences documenting the social and military conflict in El Salvador have prompted his decision to enroll at The Club. He explains that he desired to be emersed in an environment where violence is only symbolic, where the submissive individual is never actually harmed, and where violence is subject to coherent restrictions. While in El Salvador, he and some colleagues were apprehended on the street after curfew and were almost executed. Elliot is stunned to learn that his status as a journalist and as an American are not enough to save him from summary execution. Only luck and chance are his guards. Indeed, he finds out after the event that a Salvadorean national who was detained during the incident was executed while in the custody of the guards. Elliot's own nearness to death inspired the personal crisis that led him to The Club.

Elliot's account reveals society's hypocrisy regarding violence and sex. Elliot documents the atrocities of war and civil strife. His first book was a photodiary of the conflict in Beirut, and his brush with death in El Salvador occurs while he is trying to make a record of the events in that country. A journalist must document civil conflict dispassionately. However, the objective distance between Elliot and the subject of his work collapses when he almost becomes a victim. He recognizes that war is the utter abandonment of structures and standards of civility. He is attracted to The Club because it is a licensed environment where aggressions are played out with utter abandon, where there is no emotion or personal involvement. The hypocrisy lies in American culture's attitude toward these two environments. War is institutionally sanctioned and is displayed in graphic detail on the front of every newspaper. American society is inundated with violence. But sex, particularly deviant sex that mixes eroticism and violence, remains buried under a culturally imposed silence. Elliot can document his discoveries in Beirut and El Salvador in as much bloody detail as he desires, but the management of The Club takes every precaution to exclude the working investigative journalist from the environment because to divulge the activities at the resort would create a public scandal. The cultural irony lies in the fact that the society, in its hierarchy of values, prioritizes death and destruction over sex. Elliot cannot publish a photodiary of his escapades at the recreational resort. Such explicitness on a taboo subject would be a violation of socially and historically constituted standards of taste. This philosophical irony in American perceptions of sex and death is reinforced by the textual allusions to Jack Kerouac and his colleagues (*Exit* 250–51). The issue was a favorite of both the beatnik and the hippie movements, in which Rice was not always a sympathetic participant.

The author understands the paradoxical phenomenon whereby society licenses morally questionable activities within a particular space and at a particular time to facilitate transgressions of its own rules. The carnival was a public catharsis of naked aggression that is sanctioned by the very powers that would usually find its irreverence, chaotic sexualities, and abandonment of behavioral norms a threat to its sovereignty. It is a form of social control despite its promise to overthrow order and stability. The spatial and temporal boundaries of transgression created by the carnival's official sanction constituted both the promise of liberty and the control of that liberty. The very actions that undermine authority also affirm it. This is represented in Rice's novel through the spatializing of transgression. Societies license all types of barbaric aggressions and behaviors during a time of war. These actions would inspire the most severe punishment that society can impose if perpetrated during a time of peace. However, within the war zone, that same behavior is not only acceptable, but it is laudable and legitimized by the highest honors that a society can award, such as medals for valor and honor. Power structure normalizes violence within the particular area of war, but the transgression is limited by space (the locale of the war) and time (the duration of the conflict). When a society licenses violence, conflict ceases to be a threat; rules and limits rehabilitate danger. As long as violence is elevated by ritual and limitation, it is socially acceptable.

The riotous sexuality of The Club is contained upon the island in the same way that violence is sanctioned, liberated, and restrained by the politicized space of war. The boundaries of the resort and the season mark the extent of the sexual transgression. Thus, its subversive potential is normalized within the designated space and not permitted to extend beyond that area. The very same boundaries that indicate the permissibility of deviant sexuality also mark the farthest extent of its proliferation.

Obviously, S & M is the visual figuration of this paradox. The sadomasochistic body is the site of sexual liberation, but it is confined by the very real boundaries of leather straps. Lisa is an expert at sustaining and thus controlling sexual excitement in her partners, and the activities at the resort constitute the enclosure of energies that threaten to blow the place apart. However, because they are given a controlled and tempered outlet, they are rendered harmless.

The obvious parallel to this environment of simultaneous freedom and control is the French Quarter in New Orleans, the setting for a substantial portion of the novel. Many cities allow the proliferation of morally questionable activities within a designated area to allow distance from "respectable society." This allowance is a form of control. In the city of New Orleans, the transgressive space is limited to the ten-block radius of the French Quarter, where the holiday is virtually continuous. Of course, the yearly carnival Mardi Gras cannot be fully contained by the spatial boundaries of the French Quarter, and it spills out into many of the surrounding areas. One might regard the boundaries of the festival to be those of the city limits. The highly moralistic people of the Deep South can travel to New Orleans for carnival release. They may temporarily participate in the debauchery and voyeurism of the event and then return to their Bible Belt homes, safe in the knowledge that the riot is contained within the city on the coast. The city's very location suggests its marginality within regional values. It clings to the fringe of the continent. Moreover, Mardi Gras is controlled temporally by the beginning of Lent (Greenblatt 68). At midnight on Ash Wednesday, mounted police disperse the party.

Many of these events and their cultural contexts are represented in Rice's novel. Lisa and Elliot fly from the resort to New Orleans and find accommodations in the French Quarter. Their departure from The Club ironically liberates them from the communal values of that environment. The only fantasy that cannot be facilitated on the island is a lasting, monogamous, emotional bond between two people. Upon their arrival in the city, they immediately assume a more conventional sex life, a relationship characterized by equity. Moreover, gone are the whips and chains of S & M. Although crossing the borders of the island resort constitutes a shift in values, the arrival in the Big Easy certainly is not an introduction to conventional American sexual mores. Bourbon Street is itself a place of transgression, characterized by public drunkenness, riotous parties, strip shows, peep shows, gay bars, and leather, voodoo, and novelty shops. However, Lisa and Elliot are free of the unique strictures of The Club, free to pursue a relationship. They are liberated from the confines of one carnival environment and caught up in another.

Despite the conventionality of the love story, the escape from Eden does not constitute a condemnation of its practices. Lisa and Elliot reaffirm their respect for The Club's project after they have left. In their explanation, they delineate the relationship between sex and war, between The Club and the carnival, and between The Club and New Orleans. Elliot defends the actions of The Club by suggesting that the symbolic sexual violence that is normative within the space of the island is superior to the real violence that resides outside of the protective barriers of the resort. Repudiating the literal violence of the wars that he has witnessed, Elliot offers The Club as a solution to the violence that threatens to overwhelm human society:

> But there isn't any other way to save the world now, except to create arenas to work out symbolically the urges that we've taken literally in the past. Sex isn't going to go away, and neither are the destructive urges wound up in it. So if there was a Club on every street corner, if there were a million safe places in which people could act out their fantasies, no matter how primitive or repulsive, then who knows what the world would be? Real violence might become for everybody a vulgarity, an obscenity [222–23].

Elliot longs for a reversal of values, in which sex would be recognized as therapeutic and violence would be universally condemned. Here, the author brings the reader close to the theory of the carnival. The universal release of the carnival was therapeutic in the defusing of violent aggressions. The festival acted as a safety valve through which the same popular energies that might result in political insurrection or subversion could be harmlessly emancipated within the playful, irreverent atmosphere. In theory, the people who were allowed to flaunt their disrespect for the prevailing power structure would be purged of their aggressions and would resume their lives as obedient social subjects (Greenblatt 66). Similarly, at the end of *Exit to Eden*, the reader is led to believe that the S & M games are over for Lisa and Elliot. They choose a conventional lifestyle as a monogamous, married couple. Although Lisa will not return to her job on the island, she will be kept on the payroll as a consultant. The symbolic violence of The Club purged them of deviant desires and made them into normative sexual categories.

I now turn to a topic that was created in the opening paragraph of the novel: the implication of the reading audience in the activities of the exotic island and the postulating of the novel itself as a significant presence within its own narrative. At the conclusion of the first chapter, Lisa welcomes the reader to The Club, as if the reader were going to participate in the events that transpire (2). The direct address of her invitation breaks the frame of the fictional text, acknowledging the presence of a reader and placing the writer and reader in the same ontological category as the narrator. Perhaps more than any other art form, erotica invites the reader to share the activities of the characters, thus collapsing the boundary between the fictional and the real. Plainly, it is meant to sexualize the consumer, making him actually experience the excitement shared by the fictional characters. The mind of the reader becomes the island playground.

The textual allusions to Kubla Khan and Xanadu solicit this reading of the novel. In Coleridge's *Kubla Khan*, the geography of Xanadu is the geography of the mind. The walled city of the Eastern ruler contains all sensual pleasures. Moreover, the poem includes references to the unity of sensuality and violence: the "demon lover" and Kubla Khan himself. Finally, the reader of Coleridge's poem learns that the exotic paradise is only a drug-induced dream of the poem's speaker and author.

I have discussed the transgressive space, the enclosed area in which fantasy, subversion, and carnival are encouraged, contained, and rendered harmless. Have we not, all along, been talking about the enclosed area of the human mind? After all, meaning is in the mind and not on the page. The carnival has been generated in the subjective realm through the medium of language. The sexual arousal of the novel has been materially realized in the stimulation of the audience. Such a reading encourages us to reconsider the imagery of voyeurism, of the gaze that is so prevalent within the novel. The reader takes his place among the witnesses of the island's great spectacles and invites the participants into the chamber of the mind for a brief, private tryst. But how are we to read the ideology of the carnival from this perspective? How does the central thrust of the novel that we have taken such pains to delineate apply to this contracting of the novel's space?

Actually, the subjectifying of the book's content reveals a unique authorial project. Rice has emphasized the importance of liberation and play in the construction of obedient social subjects and in the elimination of literal violence within the social sphere. She offers the solution that a Club on every corner would serve to defuse the negative aggressions of the populace, rendering the people docile. Is not that exactly what she is trying to achieve by publishing her erotica? She isolates language and mind as the space in which to live the subversive dreams and symbolic violence that is so necessary for the eradication of literal violence. The novel itself becomes the enabler of such fantasies. Because the restrictive morality of the American public will not permit the construction of places such as The Club, Rice has offered an alternative. In an important passage, she emphasizes the significance of her project: "They can't sanitize or legislate our sexuality out of us. It's got to be understood and contained" (224). The novel offers a compelling argument for the importance of the imaginary life. The power structure will not permit people to act out their darkest sexual fantasies, so the only safe place is within the subjective space of human consciousness. Dreams are generated and have their impact, liberating the pent-up frustrations and aggressions. However, they are also rendered harmless. The limits of the human mind mark both the licensed space within which transgression can exist and the full extent of its growth.

The images that began the essay can be viewed in a new light. Rice was overjoyed that she had published *Exit to Eden* in hardcover in the United States, implying that such an act was a breach of normative standards of decency (Ramsland *Prism* 235). In other words, she boasts that her project has been successful in conveying an important message to a population that Freud characterized as "despicably moralistic" about sex (quoted in Abelove 386). She has presented to them a novel that is likely to offend their sense of decorum and propriety, but she has offered it in a form that encourages them to give it due consideration. In addition, the hardcover edition undermines the subversive, offensive content of the novel by placing it within the boundaries of the publishing industry's standards of acceptability. The carnivalesque content of the novel that threatens to overwhelm American morality is limited to the space defined for it by the economic system. Publishing the novel between hardcovers enhances the likelihood of its success. In America, success is measured entirely by finances. Thus, if the novel is successful, it becomes a capitulation to the values perpetuated by the power structure. Specifically, the valve is materialism, that carnival of consumer goods that makes all of us numb, content, comfortable, and obedient.

Rice viewed *Exit to Eden* as a "heightened form of porn" (Ramsland *Prism* 228). Just what does this mean to us? Our society defines obscenity as sexually explicit material that has "no redeeming social value." Such a statement cannot be made about Rice's novel. If we accept the author's implicit plans for the work, then we must conclude that no other novel has had such an ambitious social project. The novel is supposed to transform the reader through the cathartic release of pent-up sexual frustrations. Certainly, such a project elevates "porn."

One means of analyzing the novel's transgressive potential is to examine the changes in the narrative that Hollywood made as it attempted to transform the work into a major motion picture. Rice has not been restrained in her criticism of the film. Appearing on an episode of *Ellen*, the author indicated that Rosie O'Donnell and she have agreed not to talk about it to maintain their friendship. The ways in which the story was sanitized tells us much about the appeal of the novel to mainstream America. Perhaps most important is the imposition of an additional plot over the author's story line. One of the most common criticisms of pornography is that it has no plot. Deborah Ameron, the Hollywood screenwriter who adapted Rice's novel for film, must have felt this way about *Exit to Eden* because the additional material creates a main plot that involves a diamond heist and a pursuit of the criminal onto the island. The new plot does not simply elaborate on the preexisting narrative of the two lovers. It becomes the principal focus of the film. Of course, most of the sexually explicit material of the novel is either removed or altered. The slaves are not kept naked on the island but are made to wear bikini swimsuits. The S & M sex is toned down substantially, limited to a few uninteresting paddlings. All of the homoerotic material is removed. The constant eroticism of The Club is limited to sex seminars that the resort staff holds for the benefit of the guests. There are further alterations in the S & M motif of the island. The portrayals of Elliot and Lisa are modified to deemphasize the obligatory hostility between master and slave. Lisa becomes the amused, lighthearted dominatrix. Elliot is transformed into a comic, fawning, young lover without any of the tragic insight that Rice made integral to his character. Moreover, the language of slavery is removed from the script, probably so that the film will not appear to make light of the suffering of generations of Americans. The slaves of the novel are called "citizens" in the movie's dialogue.

Perhaps the most interesting addition to the narrative is the humor of the main plot. Bakhtin speaks at great length about the importance of laughter in the carnival tradition (59–144). Popular laughter is an important vehicle in the mockery and ridicule of the prevailing power structure that is so important to the festival inversion of authority. Garry Marshall's film of *Exit to Eden* employs laughter extensively, carnivalizing the carnival. The characters, played by Rosie O'Donnell and Dan Aykroyd, undermine the seriousness of the original plot by mocking and deriding the practices of The Club. It is true that they are the life of a film that is otherwise quite flat and dull.

The changes made in the narrative are coherent in light of American sexual morality and economic priorities. The alterations, calculated to give the film a broad appeal, capitulate to the subtle censorship of the American movie-rating system that consigns to financial failure any film that is targeted to mature audiences, those 17 and over. In this system, sex is regarded as more indecent than is graphic violence, and it is assigned the harsher ratings. An adolescent is permitted to watch the simulated violence of eviscerations and dismemberments on film, but he is not allowed to view the naked human body or the enactment of sexual intercourse. This is the very hypocrisy of American sexual morality that Rice attacks in her novel. The film then becomes the material representation of what the novel satirizes.

Much of the subversion of the text is recuperated by its recognizably conservative conclusions. Rice herself acknowledged that the novel has been offensive to some advocates of S & M because it implies that bondage is just a phase that one must overcome if the individual hopes to achieve sexual maturity and true erotic fulfillment. Lisa and Elliot, after a brief hesitation, decide to marry in spite of the deviant fantasies that they have both harbored. This resolution of their relationship seems to violate all of the principles that have thus far been articulated by the action of the novel. At the outset, both of the lovers had sworn off the opposite sex. Elliot longs to be dominated by someone as "tough as himself" (26). Lisa seems to be similarly committed to homoeroticism. She is involved with the slave Diana, who begins to sulk as soon as her mistress becomes fascinated with Elliot. Ironically, the unconventionality of the two lover's sexual orientation is not nurtured within the atmosphere of The Club, but it is instead thwarted. The novel suggests that if two such people meet in an environment of complete openness, an environment where they can get in touch with their repressed sexual fantasies, they will discover that it was the bourgeois dream of marriage and commitment that they always desired. It suggests that alternative sexual identities are only a phase to be traversed on the road to real fulfillment in a normative relationship. Thus, it reinforces the cultural mandate for sexual uniformity and constitutes a capitulation to the very same value system that it claims to transgress.

The reader is introduced to Lisa's repressed desire to be what the world calls normal: "I will fall in love, get married, have children. I will, I will" (86–87). Although she does not again state this desire, she does, at least at the subconscious level, attempt to actualize it. She is ultimately successful. Despite her recognition that "normal" is a constituted value system that has no validity beyond a particular set of social, historical, and economic circumstances, Lisa evidently harbors a very strong desire to realize a conventional relationship. Similarly, Elliot is warned by his trainer, Martin, that he may be looking for an individual instead of a system like The Club, but the slave assures him otherwise. The swiftness with which Elliot bonds with Lisa is evidence that Martin was correct in his warning; Elliot had not actually known what he desired most. The transgressive potential of The Club is rehabilitated by an essentialist doctrine that assumes all people have the same needs and values. Sometimes, however, they require an extraordinary set of circumstances to facilitate their demands.

The implicit psychological attraction of these two characters to each other seems simple enough, and it reinforces the presumption that people who are committed to homoerotic relationships have had a painful experience with a member of the opposite gender or have not yet met the right person. Elliot desires to couple with men because he wants someone as strong as himself. Plainly, he finds that person in Lisa. She does, after all, dominate him for a substantial portion of the novel. On the other hand, Lisa requires a submissive male, but not one who is so easily tamed, and she finds that in Elliot. She is immediately attracted to the photo in his file because he does not seem to be intimidated by his situation. Yet her desire for him peaks when he becomes frightened at the whipping post and begs her to remove his blindfold. If the novel were to leave these two in the midst of gender reversals, it would promote potentially subversive sexual politics, but it does not. The inversions of The Club are only temporary, and their limits are marked by the borders of the island. Once Elliot and Lisa arrive in New Orleans, they become gender stereotypes. Lisa becomes weak and effeminate, sulking and experiencing guilt, while Elliot consoles her, assuming the role of the strong, masculine presence. Rice suggests that as long as The Club's rules and rituals suppress emotions, the two characters can assume social roles that are less common to their gender. However, once they are liberated from those particular restraints upon their behavior, they will assume conventional positions within the sociosexual hierarchy. This is an essentialist conclusion that is hostile to contemporary theories about gender construction.

Another recuperation of the novel's subversive program involves the politics of class. The carnival was often the site of the class struggle between the "laboring poor" and the "wealthy landowners" (Stallybrass and White 16). The popular riot of the festival period was calculated to demonstrate the fictionality of the social hierarchy through the satire and parody of the social elite (Stallybrass and White 19). In Rice's novel, the primacy of the traditional class structure is reaffirmed. Indeed, the island resort can be viewed as a "microcosm of society" (Ramsland *Prism* 226). Although the magnificent bodies of the slaves are the objects of the gaze and admiration of the wealthy members, the slaves are nonetheless in a position of subordination to the monied class, which exploits them,

humiliates them, and regards them as objects to be manipulated for pleasure. Money and influence are the only means of gaining access to The
Club's membership. The poor can only participate as slaves, surrendering
their freedom and their bodies for substantial rewards. The novel allego-
rizes hegemony: domination through the consent of the dominated. Marxist theory regards capitalism as a form of slavery in which the slave has a
license to sell his labor to whomever she chooses, but she must sell it to
someone. On the other hand, the wealthy, the owners of the means of production, are entitled to the surplus of the individual's labor, thereby guar-
anteeing the continued submission of the subordinate, who will never be
able to afford independence. The slaves on the island are never going to
amass enough wealth to join the club as members. They are paid only a
modest sum $50,000 per year, for the use of their bodies, which can assure
comfort so long as one continues to labor, but it offers no long-term economic security.

　　The carnival games on the island are designed to humiliate and dehu-
manize the slaves. In one game, rings are tossed around the heads of the
participants. In another game, felt balls are thrown at Velcro strips that
are fastened to the naked buttocks of the bound slaves. The poor are
obliged to degrade themselves, to offer their bodies to sustain the wealth
and pleasure of the rich. Of course, in this reading, the sexual imagery
represents the literal and figurative domination that is implicit within the
class structures. There is one important exception to this rule, and that is
Elliot. He is wealthy, but he has opted to enter the resort as a slave. He
is there not for money but for pleasure. However, even he relies upon his
wealth to overcome his submission. He flies off to New Orleans to live it
up for a few days and then returns to The Club as a member. This episode
only reinforces the class distinctions because Elliot, a rich man in a
laborer's world, is the only one to escape. The social inversion of the
medieval carnival is reversed once again. Social hierarchies are shown to
be unassailable. The wealthy are predominant in The Club's environment,
while the poor are satirized and parodied. Even Lisa assumes a servile
role in relation to the members, facilitating their every desire.

　　The containment of the novel's attack on religion is enabled by the
same apparatus that is intended to subvert. The inclusion of religious
imagery in the description of the resort only succeeds in characterizing
The Club's atmosphere as the demonized opposite of Christian sexual
ethics. Even Lisa cannot decide whether the resort is heaven or hell. To
appropriate the language of religion is to affirm its authority in determining values and lifestyles. Moreover, the escape and subsequent marriage of the two protagonists at the end of the novel reasserts the primacy

of conventional attitudes about sexual morality, which the power structure and its chief ideological and hegemonic mouthpiece, the Christian Church, have perpetrated.

Finally, one might wonder why the author would choose to promote an orthodox discourse on sex in her conclusion. Perhaps it is creative license, a random product of the vicissitudes of the artistic process, or it may be a capitulation to the standards of popular taste that is intended to facilitate the novel's financial success. The latter seems more likely because similar conservative conclusions can be observed in most of the author's works. Is it any wonder then that the novel reinforces bourgeois interests? The author is even fashioning herself as a full participant in American materialism and the capitalist quest for profits. Of course, in her defense, one could argue that if she were really interested in exorbitant profit margins, she would not choose to write erotica. This interpretive conflict may be resolved by regarding the novel as a compromise between the demands of the marketplace and artistic creativity.

Chapter 6

PRURIENT PAINTERS AND PEDOPHILES: NEGOTIATING CONSENT IN *BELINDA*

Anne Rice may have had good reason to publish her erotica under her two pseudonyms, Anne Rampling and Anne Roquelaure. Four of the five books depict the sexual practices of adolescent boys and girls, and these depictions followed close behind the kiddie-porn panic of the late 1970s, in which right-wing demagogs attempted to incite parents into a homophobic hysteria by suggesting that gay men and women were attempting to lure children into deviant sexual practices, prostitution, and pornography. During this period, laws were enacted to protect children from the predacious sexual behavior of adults, making it illegal to photograph a naked child. At the same time, written publications that advocated intergenerational relations were closed down and prosecuted under obscenity laws (Califia 41–45).

The recent controversy over the remake of the film *Lolita* demonstrates that the cultural hysteria over the potential pollution of the young has not diminished in the past twenty years. *Lolita*, starring Jeremy Irons, was not released in theaters in the United States as it was in Britain. Instead, it appeared on cable television where, ironically, access to its content could not be regulated at all. Perhaps the refusal of theaters to market the film constitutes a moral victory for the self-appointed protectors of the American conscience, because the decision removed the subject from the public arena and placed it entirely within the private realm, the home. In a sense, the process then became one of sublimation in which the offending material was to be relegated to the cultural unconscious. The material can be viewed, but it cannot be acknowledged publicly. This cultural process of driving the illicit underground, particularly in this instance, legitimizes the practice that it intends to repudiate. Molestation, contrary to popular belief, is primarily the problem of the home and the family. The overwhelming number of cases of child molestation occur within the context of the father-daughter relationship. Thus, the consigning of the offending material to the discretion of the parents and to the privacy of the home encourages the secrecy that makes molestation feasible. It ostensibly respects the very authority that should be suspected.

American culture and media constantly rouses prurient interest in the eroticized bodies of adolescent girls. In the 1970s, the controversy was over the propriety of allowing a model as young as Brooke Shields to be paraded in front of the American public as an object of desire or of making a movie such as *Blue Lagoon*, which despite the ad campaign characterizing the innocent and natural love of the two children marooned on the tropical island, nevertheless offered up naked adolescents to the lascivious gaze of the entire adult population (Kincaid 364). The practice of choosing teenage girls as the representatives of beauty and desirability encourages the very practice that the culture ostensibly reviles. More recently, the use of adolescent girls in ads for companies such as Calvin Klein have fueled controversy. One such ad was so suggestive that it prompted the angry commentary of President Clinton, who labeled the ad "disgusting" and protested that the girl depicted in the suggestive pose was as young as his daughter.

Rice's erotica, which frequently focuses on the sexuality of adolescents, was published in the midst of the notorious censorship scandals of the 1980s, but it prompted admiration as opposed to condemnation. In her biography, Rice admits that her publisher begged her not to release the *Erotic Adventures of Sleeping Beauty*, fearing that it would ruin her reputation as a writer (Riley 46). She adds triumphantly that the novels have only improved her literary prestige, and it is indeed true that her erotica is some of her most highly regarded work.

Belinda (1986) was the last of the five erotic novels to be published. The subject matter is a thinly veiled allegory of the problems and risks that Rice had in her efforts to publish her Rampling and Roquelaure novels (Riley 45). In the novel, Jeremy Walker, a painter and renowned author of children's books, meets Belinda, a very mature sixteen-year-old girl whom he embraces as a lover. He also adopts her as the subject of a series of nude paintings that constitute a professional breakthrough and triumph for the artist. However, Jeremy is aware that exhibiting his work in public could result in the discovery of his sexual involvement with Belinda and lead to his prosecution on charges of statutory rape.

The bare outline of the novel includes a number of glaring similarities to Rice's real predicament as an author. She recognized that her erotic novels were a professional milestone and a departure from her usual work and that they could be instrumental in improving her reputation as a serious writer. However, she was also afraid that they could damage her professionally if the public were to determine that they were obscene or dangerous. Just as Jeremy was urged by friends and publishers not to exhibit his nude paintings because they would create a backlash against his children's books, Rice's publisher pleaded with her not to release the novels even under a pseudonym, fearing that they would decrease the marketability of her horror fiction. The eventual display of Jeremy's breakthrough work does result in the burning of his children's books throughout the Bible Belt, but it also results in his recognition as an important American painter. As a result of his personal courage, his paintings end up in important museums throughout the world. Similarly, Rice decided to reveal her authorship of the Rampling and Roquelaure novels with the publication of *Belinda*, perhaps because it had become clear that the public approved of the novels. Also, the author may have decided that, as in the novel, the potential for artistic immortality was more compelling than was the desire to maintain the good opinion of uptight sexual conservatives.

Despite the boldness of her decision to reveal her authorship, Rice is preoccupied with the impact of the sex scandal upon the professional careers of the participants in *Belinda*, particularly because the scandal involves an adult and a minor. This issue becomes a leitmotif within the novel. In addition to the scandal that Jeremy's painting creates, Belinda's precocious sensuality has created problems elsewhere. She had a small part in an independent film titled *Final Score*, in which she is depicted in a lesbian sexual encounter. The film, made by Susan Jeremiah, an exciting young director, received considerable recognition at Cannes. Belinda, despite her small part in the production, became the darling of the festival. However, the film is not initially well received by American distributors. Belinda's stepfather, Marty, kills the distribution contract for the production, suggesting that he does not want Belinda to be introduced to the American movie audience with a lesbian scene. Thus, he feigns concern for her acting career while, in reality, he is attempting to rescue his popular prime-time soap, which stars Belinda's mother, Bonnie Blanchard. Marty fears that if Bonnie's daughter is implicated in a public scandal, the uproar will affect the television show's ratings. Indeed, it is true that when the scandal involving Jeremy's paintings breaks, the show, *Champaign Flight*, is canceled. The television program's content appropriately resembles the real predicament of its star. Bonnie's character is a corporate executive who is being blackmailed by a cousin because she once made erotic films.

Marty's reputation and career are also compromised. His affair with Belinda has been discovered by his wife, the girl's mother. Of course, the shallow, self-centered mother is only angry about her daughter's betrayal, subsequently driving her out of the house at gunpoint. Although Belinda admits that she was the aggressor, with minors there can be no legal consent, so Marty is guilty of statutory rape. The revelation of his involvement with his stepchild is another of the eventualities that sinks his prime-time soap. Even if his involvement with a minor as emotionally mature as Belinda is not enough to turn the readers of the novel against Marty, his efforts to destroy the careers and reputations of others should finish the task. Belinda's real father, GG, is a gay hairdresser in New York. Marty circulates a rumor that an employee of GG has AIDS. The resulting rash of cancellations jeopardizes GG's salon. Angry with his efforts to destroy those whom she loves, Belinda repeatedly threatens to reveal her involvement with Marty. Nevertheless, she is not very successful at bringing an end to his machinations until the entire sordid affair is publicly revealed.

The text also contains multiple references to the director Roman Polanski, whose career was ruined when his affair with an adolescent girl was discovered. He was forced to leave the country to avoid prosecution. The fate of Polanski is repeatedly offered as a check on the behavior of the characters in the novel. Belinda refers to the wayward director when she threatens to destroy her stepfather:

> I'll put your husband in San Quentin for statutory rape on account of what happened. I'll tell the juvenile authorities everything that went on between him and me. It was unlawful intercourse with a minor in case you're interested, and if you think they drove Roman Polanski out of this town for it, you wait and see what happens to Marty [328–29].

Of course, all of the discussion of reputation and career is particularly relevant to the predicament of the protagonist. Jeremy Walker is, according to law, a statutory rapist. Yet Rice is careful to diminish the association of her protagonist with predacious sexual behavior. Belinda is a sixteen-year-old girl who is financially independent, sexually aggressive, and emotionally mature enough to make her own decisions. Jeremy is not a lascivious old man determined to prey upon teenagers everywhere. In an argument with his friend Alex, Jeremy maintains that careers are no longer destroyed by sex scandal as they once were, an assertion that does not prove to be entirely true within the novel. Jeremy's own career is destroyed, reshaped, and resurrected. He is subject to the outcry of conservatives, who burn his books and call him a child molester. Certainly his work as an author of children's books will never be the same after the discovery of his involvement with Belinda and the public realization that all along he had a prurient interest in his characters and, perhaps, even in the readers of his books. Thus, the novel becomes the story of an artist's evolution. He leaves behind children's literature to pursue serious art with mature content.

The mitigating circumstance that makes Belinda's sexual precocity acceptable within the context of the novel and that impedes the reader's condemnation of Jeremy is the emotional independence of Belinda. Rice has been very bold in her advocacy of an adolescent's right to pursue an object of desire, even one considerably older than herself (Riley 53). Of course, this does not include an endorsement of child molestation, but it calls for a reevaluation of the age of consent. Rice protests that age-of-consent laws are not hard and fast indicators of an adolescent's readiness for sexual initiation. The age of consent varies from country to country and even from state to state. Thus, the culture cannot agree on the time at which children are prepared for carnal knowledge. Rice even offers the sexual aggression of adolescents as a mitigating circumstance in situations involving statutory rape, a circumstance to which the law is blind.

Rice makes a considerable effort to portray Belinda as sufficiently mature to negotiate an erotic relationship with an adult the age of Jeremy. Belinda is already living independently of her family when she meets Jeremy. More important to the redemption of Jeremy's character, Belinda already experienced her sexual awakening long before she met him and with several separate partners. She has also appeared in a movie involving a lesbian sex scene and has actually been intimate with the female director. She has had an affair with an Arab prince whom she met in Europe, and she has been previously involved with her stepfather, who clearly did not care about her. So by the time that Jeremy meets her, she is not in any way sexually naive. Rice even exaggerates the character's sexual maturity, suggesting that Belinda is so comfortable with her body that she teaches Jeremy not to be ill at ease with his own. And if all of this were not enough to extenuate the circumstances surrounding Jeremy's involvement with Belinda, the author offers still another factor. Jeremy does not know how old Belinda is until after he has already become involved with her. After the relationship between the two has been exposed and has become a national scandal, Jeremy trumpets his intentions to marry Belinda as soon as she can be found. Through marriage, he hopes to avert condemnation and prosecution for his involvement with a minor. This is not to say that he does not love her or that he would not have married her under better circumstances, but he does broach the idea when his future freedom seems to be most in jeopardy.

In her book *Public Sex*, Pat Califia argues for the merits of inter-generational relationships by suggesting that the adult partner frequently constitutes a surrogate parent. Califia adds that such relationships are not always destructive and that they can offer emotional and financial sup-port that the minor cannot get at home (62–68). Similarly, in his book *Erotics and Politics*, author Tim Edwards distinguishes between the tra-ditions of pederasty and pedophilia and the modern concept of the child molester. The latter is an invention that is subsequent to the compara-tively recent construction of modern childhood, which scholars attribute to nineteenth-century industrialism and the rise of the modern middle class. Many children were released from their former obligation to labor in factories, and the contemporary concept of the innocent, idle child was born. With this concept came the molester, who preyed upon the vul-nerability of the child and whose actions were entirely self-serving and destructive. Pederasty, out of the Greek tradition, was frequently an edu-cational arrangement, while pedophilia involved a nurturing, often exclu-sive relationship between an adult and a child (55–61). The practices of pederasty and pedophilia were not always construed as hurtful to the child. It is this type of relationship that Rice portrays in *Belinda*.

Certainly, Rice has taken great pains to demonstrate that her young protagonist is better off in the company of Jeremy than with a self-serv-ing mother. Jeremy immediately assumes a paternal role with Belinda. After a disturbance in a neighboring apartment, the police interrogate Belinda because they are convinced that she is not old enough to be liv-ing on her own. She tries to rescue her independence by telling them that Jeremy is her father, and he arrives to reinforce the sham and to rescue Belinda from protective custody.

Rice protests that the public cannot even conceptualize a relation-ship between an adult and an adolescent that is not destructive: "[Y]ou won't even settle for anything between a man and a girl her age that was just plain wholesome and good" (428). She further ridicules this narrow-mindedness by observing the frequent association of sex with death in the minds of the public. Alex reminds Jeremy that death accompanied explicit sexual narratives in popular culture because death offers an appropriate penalty for sexual license in the minds of the public. The novel *Belinda* illustrates this expectation in its own narrative. After the scandal is revealed and Belinda disappears, the media and the authorities immediately assume that Jeremy has murdered his young lover. The public expectation of the child molester is that he will defile his victim and then kill her. The police even begin a investigation and are ready to make an arrest of the painter when Belinda finally resurfaces. The final painting in the Belinda series, *The Artist Grieves for Belinda*, is even interpreted as a manifestation of the painter's presumed guilt over the murder of his mistress. The public expectation, however, is frustrated when the presumed murder victim shows up at the San Francisco premiere of *Final Score*, a film that was criticized for not offering the appropriate moral index to remind the audience that unrestrained, forbidden sex should not go unpunished. The director, Susan Jeremiah, promises producers that her next film will be "puritanically based" and that "[a]ll the sex we'd show would be bad" (298).

Rice dallies with the presumption that sex will lead to violent death to impeach social and literary expectations. The forbidden sex between Belinda and Jeremy is neither destructive nor hurtful in the expected way. However, considering how much Jeremy suffers in both his career and his personal life, one cannot say that his transgression has gone unpunished. Nevertheless, the relationship ultimately proves beneficial for both Belinda and Jeremy. Belinda is no longer on the run, and Jeremy has achieved an artistic breakthrough and a wife. Despite the sex, one cannot argue that Belinda would be better off at home.

Belinda's mother is clearly not a fit guardian. She is extraordinarily self-centered, destroying her daughter's movie career when it jeopardizes her own. She discovers an illicit affair between her husband Marty and her underaged daughter and blames the girl so as not to destroy a professionally advantageous marriage. She openly admits that she attempted to shoot her daughter when she discovered the affair. Bonnie also blackmails Jeremy. This crime is neither for money nor for the return of her daughter, but to guarantee that Belinda stays with Jeremy until she is 18. These circumstances guarantee that she would not return home to become her mother's burden. To further undermine the reader's sympathy for Bonnie, the author makes her profoundly hypocritical. After the daughter's affair with Jeremy is exposed nationally, Bonnie feigns devastation over the news, posing as a caring parent who desires justice against child molesters. Even when her daughter phones to tell her that she is not dead, Bonnie refuses to abandon her pose as the distraught mother. Instead, she hangs up and states that the caller is not her child.

Rice further reinforces her socially iconoclastic perspective on children's welfare by negating the destructive myths surrounding gay parenthood.

Standard homophobic rants suggest that gay parents are irresponsible, incapable of abandoning the narcissistic pursuit of pleasure long enough to focus on the welfare of a child. In *Belinda*, Rice has invested these negative qualities in the mother, the person most often relied upon for nurturing. Belinda's gay father is far more considerate of his daughter's welfare than is her mother. Although GG's complicity in the relationship between Belinda and Jeremy comes dangerously close to the mythic alliance between gays and pedophiles, the novel avoids homophobia by making the mother's collusion greater. In the inverted morality of the novel, those individuals most often associated with the child's well-being are vilified and the usual scapegoats absolved.

The author also toys with the mitigating factor of adolescent sexual aggression. Rice has maintained elsewhere that the child's initiation of a sexual encounter with an adult is an extenuating circumstance. There is no uniformity in the emotional development of adolescents. Some may be mature enough to navigate a sexual encounter with an adult, while the majority may not be. However, the law is uniform, criminalizing all sexual contact between adults and teenagers or between two teenagers (Ramsland *Prism* 52). The sexually aggressive behavior of Belinda, coupled with her former experiences, is supposed to rescue Jeremy from the stigma of molester and pedophile. She has been the initiator in at least two sexual encounters with adults, Jeremy and Marty, and her erotic experiences are even more numerous. The politics of this particular aspect of the narrative are suspect. While our culture criminalizes erotic acts between children and adults, dispensing with even the possibility of consent, it also recognizes variations in culpability that are determined by an evaluation of the adolescent's former sexual experience. For example, young girls who run away from home and make their living through prostitution are less likely to inspire the wrath of the law than are middle-class girls who have little or no sexual experience and are seduced by a friend's father. The law evaluates, even if unconsciously, the level of pollution inherent in the adolescent's person. Jeremy is less of a threat to teenage girls if Belinda has slept around.

The implicit, sometimes explicit evaluation of adolescents' sexual experience has a profoundly sexist implication as well. When the subject is a teenage boy, the legal system seems less eager to evaluate the child's previous experience, particularly when the incident involves a same-sex encounter (Tsang 8). An event that occurred in Philadelphia in the early 1990s made national headlines and confirmed this heterosexist double standard. An adult male who was HIV positive was caught soliciting the sexual favors of adolescent boys. The initial hysteria over the culprit's activities resulted from the conjunction of three of the public's most profound fears: the fear of gay men's sexual appetites, the fear of the pollution of children, and the fear of the mythic AIDS predator. Initially, the culprit was accused of intentionally infecting the boys and was denied bail. Authorities completely absolved the boys of any responsibility for the situation at the same time that they very delicately explained the boys had been accepting cash for sexual favors. The term "prostitution" was not used to describe the boys' behavior. In the eyes of the public, they were innocent of their own sexual history and were the unwitting victims of a predacious sexual appetite. Had the victim been a female, there is little doubt that she would have been labeled a whore and dismissed for having brought about own her suffering. In all likelihood, she would have been assumed to be the source of the infection. The adult male was eventually granted a very substantial bail after his lawyers argued that the original denial assumed that he was guilty before being proven so.

Age-of-consent and statutory-rape laws are designed to protect children from the rapacious sexual behavior of adults. The law assumes that children and adolescents are powerless and easily exploited by their elders. However, as a consequence of these laws, children are invested with a prodigious amount of power over adults. In most cases, it is a power that children have no capacity to appreciate or manipulate. The mere accusation of impropriety with a child can destroy a career or a reputation, and a conviction on such a charge can result in prison terms more lengthy than those dealt out to some murderers (Califia 53). Moreover, as in cases of sexual harassment, the burden of proof is turned on its head. The accused is placed in the untenable position of proving that she did not commit the crime, whereas in other cases the accuser is obliged to prove the charges.

In cases of suspected child abuse, there is an assumption of guilt that sometimes cannot be shaken even when the accusations become patently absurd or when the suspect is absolved of guilt. Witness the McMartin Preschool scandal. Parents and authorities took the veracity of the children for granted even when the kids told stories of being taken in airplanes, subjected to satanic rituals, or perhaps even more remarkable, of being molested by middle-aged and elderly women, a group not generally considered a threat to children (Kincaid 382).

Belinda is conscious of the power that she has over adults, and her ability to manipulate that power is the clearest sign that she is mature enough to navigate a relationship with an older man. She laments that scandal follows her, destroying everyone she meets. Her involvement with Susan Jeremiah results in the loss of the filmmaker's distribution contract for *Final Score*. Her father GG's business is destroyed by those eager to control Belinda. Jeremy loses his career as a children's author and almost sacrifices his freedom.

Paradoxically, the same laws intended to protect Belinda succeed in criminalizing her. Age-of-consent laws make it illegal for adolescents to engage in sexual behavior even with children their own age. Rice's novel is cognizant of how these laws work against the very people they are designed to protect. Belinda's Uncle Daryl has the Los Angeles Police Department issues a warrant for her arrest, stating that "she is a minor without proper supervision, leading an immoral and dissolute life" (428). The scandal over her involvement with Jeremy results in such a sensation that she becomes the object of the prurient gaze of the entire country. Her disappearance results in a nationwide manhunt, replete with the televised appeals of loved ones requesting her return. The process of trying to protect her turns out to be the most damaging aspect of the entire episode. Ironically, it necessitates that she be accepted as an adult by ensuring her marriage to Jeremy and by continuing her movie career. The people who are ostensibly trying to help Belinda (her mother and her Uncle Daryl) are the ones who are most responsible for making her life a scandalous front-page story.

The public attention riveted on Belinda raises another very contentious issue: child pornography. The scandal involving Jeremy and Belinda would not have been so transgressive had it not been for the 18 nude paintings of Belinda that Jeremy completed during the affair. The paintings have a paradoxical effect upon the public. Those who know and understand art recognize the works as masterpieces, but those preoccupied with the sexual innocence of children regard them as "kiddie porn." The campaign to eradicate children's pornography in the late 1970s resulted in a series of laws, one of which made it a felony, even for parents, to photograph or film nude children (Califia 42). The controversy over the Robert Mapplethorpe exhibit in Cincinnati and the subsequent obscenity trial suggest that the outrage over the depiction of nude children has persisted. With her novel *Belinda*, Rice argues that images of naked children are not automatically prurient or pornographic. The author has made considerable effort to show that Jeremy's paintings have enormous artistic content, a factor that is intended to negate the charge of indecency. Jeremy defends his work, maintaining that the paintings were supposed to be "wholesome and beautiful" (427).

The censorship trials during the 1980s revealed a dichotomy in public opinion similar to that represented in the novel. The moralists and religious hysterics who have little love for, and even less knowledge of, art are pitted against defenders of free speech and art critics, the people most qualified to determine the aesthetic content of a creative production. The same forces are at work in the novel. Jeremy's paintings create a stir of excitement in the artistic community, selling for up to $500,000 each once they are finally displayed. One canvas is even purchased for the permanent collection of the New York Metropolitan Museum of Art. The acquisition is defended by the director, who protests that his job is to identify and acquire exceptional art, not to make an assessment of the creator's morality. Rice seems to be particularly offended by the complicity of feminism in the campaign to eradicate pornography. She has repeatedly attacked feminist groups who side with the Moral Majority, suggesting that they are antiwoman and that women have a right to own their sexual appetites no matter how voracious those might be (Ramsland *Prism* 218).

The greatest offense of the paintings is not that they are obscene, but that the existence of the paintings leads to a reinterpretation and reevaluation of Jeremy's books. The prurient interest in the adolescent body represented in the paintings suggests that the author may have had a hidden desire all along for the children he portrayed and entertained. Moreover, his seemingly innocent work may carry secret messages that compromise his audience's virtue. The frightened children in bedclothes peering into darkened doorways, who people Jeremy's books, signify the fearful awakening of erotic desire in the pubescent child. Thus, the books constitute a preoccupation with the salacious desires of 12-year-old children. Even Jeremy's friend Alex interprets the paintings as an indication that the author had always desired to look beneath the nightgowns of his former childhood heroines.

Just as with the recent controversy over Disney productions, the public requires an unflagging confidence in those who entertain children, and even a hint of carnal desire taints the entire production. The assessment of the child's virtue involves a pair of mutually exclusive categories. Like the representations of women in Early Modern literature, the child moves directly from purity to total depravity, occupying no realistic middle ground of informed virtue. In the public mind, any taint of the child's purity is contagious, saturating the entire body, and our culture defines a child's innocence entirely in terms of the sex act. A child could be subject to the most obscene violence and still maintain her innocence, but the merest hint of carnal knowledge obliterates childhood.

In *Belinda*, Jeremy's integrity is impugned. Although the assumption that he desires to couple with adolescents can be awarded some credibility, there is no justification for assuming that his books are a danger, particularly since years of scrutiny had failed to turn up any secret sala-cious messages urging his readers toward a premature sexual awakening. Nevertheless, the explicit paintings of Belinda render suspect his previ-ous work. His books are subjected to the same scrutiny that conceptual-izes the fragile innocence of the child. He is deemed unreliable, unwor-thy of many parents' trust.

The inclusion of the child in any form of pornography compromises the innocence of all children because it renders the child's body an accept-able object for the lascivious gaze of adult males, as the sexual abuse of children is almost entirely a male phenomenon (Kincaid 15). Belinda has been compromised twice by so-called pornography: Susan Jeremiah's film and Jeremy's canvases. However, she is unaffected by the experience. Indeed, the novel indicates that the real crime is believing that the nude body is obscene. Rice takes great care to demonstrate that Belinda is not self-conscious about her body. Thus, her nude display is not a violation of her privacy and is not coerced. Moreover, Belinda is so far from any fear of exposure that she becomes infuriated when Jeremy explains that he will never display the canvases; the resulting row creates a breach that almost ends their relationship. Upon her departure, Belinda leaves explicit permission to show the work, explaining that the artist must have the courage to tell the truth: "You have made art out of what has happened. And you have earned the right to use the truth in any way that you want" (372). The settings of the paintings are intended to undermine the charge of obscenity against them. Belinda is most often represented in situations that, apart from her nudity, would be considered wholesome. She is depicted on carousel rides and at Holy Communion. In the latter, the setting does not render ironic the sacrament of Holy Communion. It reveals that Belinda's nudity is not a violation but is a continuation of that context.

Belinda is an overt attack upon the principles of the kiddie porn panic of the 1970s. It is simultaneously a defense of the artist's right to use whatever subject matter is appropriate to her project even if that mate-rial involves the depiction of children's nudity or their salacious behav-ior. The novel interrogates the assumption that all creative products that include the depiction of naked children are obscene and exploitative. This assumption would eliminate the religious and romantic art of the Renais-sance because much of it depicts naked cherubs in flight around the cen-tral figures of the paintings. *Belinda* features an adolescent who consents to pose nude for a series of paintings, who has the capacity to appreciate the outcome of her choice, and who is so far from being exploited that she encourages the display of the canvases in opposition to the artist's reticence. While Rice's decision to make Belinda 16 diminishes the radical potential of her subject, it also allows her to make her point without being dismissed out of hand. In all likelihood, few readers would have the stomach for a novel that depicts that sexual initiation of a 12-year-old girl, even a precocious 12-year-old girl. Yet the depiction of nude teenagers beneath the year of consent is nevertheless sufficiently scandalous to allow the author her challenge to propriety and convention.

As with her other novels, Rice's ostensibly revolutionary subject matter is compromised for the sake of commercialism or for moral reticence. The author admits that in the composition of the novel she acquiesced to pressure from publishers and friends to make Belinda older than was her original intent, which was a scandalous 12 years old. Such an alteration is obviously calculated to minimize the likelihood of outrage and subsequent commercial failure. The preoccupation in the novel with the sale of the paintings and the additional concern that the adolescent subject may influence their marketability reinforces this point. The artist's concern for the public acceptance of his work parallels Rice's own concern for the success of her erotica, particularly her erotica that depicts the salacious activities of boys and girls beneath the age of consent.

One can hardly impugn the author for not embracing the concept of child molestation. Belinda's age, almost 17, is at least sufficient to minimize the accusations of exploitation. However, in an effort to defend an adolescent's right to her desire, the author legitimizes sexual practices that have, in recent years, not been sufficiently interrogated. In the rush to blame gays and lesbians for all molestations, American culture has left unacknowledged and unexamined the fact that the overwhelming number of child molesters are heterosexual males. Whereas one might argue that Rice is recognizing the true sexual orientation of pedophiles with the relationship between Jeremy and Belinda, she is at the same time legitimizing the union between an adult male and an adolescent girl, the relationship that American culture already finds the most acceptable of the variations on child loving. The narrative seems to sanction the heterosexual male's historical right to define propriety in self-serving terms. From such a perspective, male homosexual practice is the "most horrid transgression under the cope of heaven," while female homosexuality is arousing. The same bias concludes that the molestation of a young girl is less worthy of public outrage than that of a young boy because the girl is being exploited in a fashion consistent with normative sexual practices.

Rice's revolutionary theories of adolescent sexuality may be precarious because they place the young adults' welfare into the hands of the most predacious element of the population: heterosexual males. Certainly, there are adolescents who are sufficiently mature to conduct themselves in a relationship with an adult, but what happens once these unions are socially and legally accepted? Who is going to evaluate the emotional maturity of the youngster? Are we going to allow the adult male to make this decision? What if he thinks that all women are docile and emotional? He may mistake confusion and naiveté for an informed and ready submissiveness. Certainly it is true that there is nothing magical about the age of 18 that transforms the teenager into an adult. However, the fact that there are varying levels of maturity in the mid-teens and that some teenagers are emotionally ready for an adult relationship also argues that some teenagers are not. The position that adolescents should be allowed to realize their desires may be a defensible one, but the argument for the lack of uniformity in the emotional maturity of teenagers refutes itself. It forgets about the element of seduction that is the largest portion of the manipulation. The seducer creates longing in the desired object. How will the adolescent know whether she is succumbing to her own desire or to that of the seducer? How will she know whether that was a choice she would have made if she was not pressured by the insistence of the seducer?

Rice has also suggested that a mitigating feature in such negotiations is the child's own seductive aggression. Once that we have acknowledged and accepted the seductive potential of adolescents, are we not opening ourselves up for the argument that she wanted it because of the way that she dressed or walked or because she flirted with the adult? The absence of consent in the litigation of child molesters is intended to emphasize that the adult has the responsibility to avoid any potentially erotic encounters with teenagers or children. The law can demand a sufficient level of maturity and self-control from an adult. It may seem here that I am taking an extraordinarily unyielding, conservative position. I do not believe that intimacy between an adult and an adolescent automatically destroys a child's life, consigning her to a life of therapy. I do not argue that adolescent sexuality should be criminalized and repressed, but the program for liberation seems fraught with the potential for abuse. The argument that a child should have the right to experiment sexually with an adult necessitates the parallel entitlement that adults should have the "right to have sex with children" (Edwards 63). The conquest of an adolescent girl is a heterosexual male fantasy and a guilty pleasure, the realization of which would restore the ancient tradition that any woman is an acceptable target for the rapacious sexual appetites of adult males.

Belinda's brief dalliance with filmmaker Susan Jeremiah reveals another small inhibition in Rice's revolutionary sexual politics. The author treats the affair as if it were merely an experiment on the part of a curious, open-minded young girl, thus reinforcing the prevalent notion that homosexual encounters are merely a phase that many young adults experience on their way to sexual maturity. This assumption has a heterosexist, paternalistic bias that is instrumental in the infantilizing and pathologizing of gays and lesbians whose relationships, with such considerations, do not need to be acknowledged or taken seriously. The affair's failure to warrant thorough commentary or to provoke the outrage of the judicial and moral authorities within the novel further reinforces the erasure of gay passion, particularly the passion between two women, which has traditionally been regarded as nonthreatening both because the phallocentric notion of sex requires a penis and because a good portion of heterosexual men find lesbian encounters arousing (Edwards 68). Belinda maintains no prolonged interest in the lesbian filmmaker, quickly abandoning her for other erotic pursuits. Jeremiah's subsequent pursuit of Belinda may be a testament to the older woman's passion, but it also characterizes gay relationships as brief, desperate, and neurotic. Jeremiah becomes the traditional homophobe's "painted devil," the sexual deviant in desperate pursuit to defile somebody's child and to make her the star of a pornographic movie.

Rice's textual negotiation between radical and capitulationist viewpoints is further developed through the absence of the explicit sexual material that is a part of her other erotic novels. Indeed, one might argue that *Belinda* is not an erotic novel at all because the descriptions of the sex act are not as detailed as they are in *Exit to Eden*, the *Sleeping Beauty* series, or even *The Lives of the Mayfair Witches*. Perhaps the author felt that the pedophilic content alone was sufficiently transgressive and that any additional provocations would arouse scandal and outrage from the reading public, perhaps even a charge of obscenity, which would lead to subsequent commercial failure. The meticulous description of the sexual encounters between an adult male and a teenage girl may have invited resistance to the serious content of the novel, which is the defense of an adolescent's sexual freedom. By provoking and tantalizing the adult reader, the novel would seem to focus on the sexual attraction of mature individuals toward adolescents rather than on the reverse.

The novel *Belinda* dramatizes a negotiation between two types of child loving: pedophilia and molestation. The former is a consenting, nurturing relationship between an adult and a child or adolescent. The latter is a destructive, nonconsensual, exploitative encounter between a criminal and an innocent. Our culture, however, refuses to recognize a distinction between the two types of perpetrators, perhaps because to legitimize the first would necessitate the recognition and acceptance of the second. Thus, there is a cultural bias against her thesis that is virtually unassailable. Legally and morally, American society refuses to recognize an adolescent's capacity to consent, and the rise of family politics has led to a hysterical, even utopian idealization of childhood innocence. National propaganda against the recognition of any difference is so pervasive and so successful that even those who may be inclined to agree with the author are frightened into silence by the potential accusation that they promote child abuse. So Rice's thesis may be somewhat compromised for the sake of public opinion, but it remains a bold and radical departure from mainstream American values, one that even this author is afraid to condone.

Chapter 7

RAPE FANTASIES: CONSTRUCTING A MASCULINE PROTOTYPE AMONG THE MAYFAIR WITCHES

Lynne Segal, in her highly regarded study of gender roles titled *Slow Motion*, observes the inevitable alterations in concepts of masculinity resulting from the women's movement. She observes that the polarization of gender roles ensures an alteration in men's behavior following the dramatic shifts in women's influence (280). The men's movement, which has been gaining much momentum over the past two decades, has begun to produce a wide variety of academic studies, most of them deconstructing the mythic inevitability of the link between sex and gender and postulating a multiplicity of male gender roles, even within the somewhat narrow range of hegemonic masculinity. These studies, often written from a pro-feminist and pro-gay perspective, attempt to dismantle the culturally constructed, limited view of masculinity that has been stigmatized as the principal source of sexual repression and persecution within Western culture. Much of this research has sought to demonstrate how narrow conceptions of masculinity have been as damaging to men as they have to women. I do not refer only to the maltreatment of gay men resulting from the often violent imposition of obligatory heterosexuality, although, of course, this is one of the chief manifestations. Instead, I refer broadly to the necessity that men attain a masculinity that is the idealized opposition to any behavior that is construed to be feminine. Such concepts of gender polarization are limiting to the practitioners who are only permitted to indulge a narrow range of experiences, particularly in the expression of emotion.

143

Anne Rice's novels seem to be particularly committed to the shattering of traditional gender constructs. We have observed this process in her representation of androgyny and in her focus on alternative sexual identities. However, in her series *The Lives of the Mayfair Witches*, Rice abandons her former fascination with the actively androgynous and the socially and sexually dissident men of the *Vampire Chronicles*, *Cry to Heaven*, and the *Beauty* series. In *The Witching Hour*, there is a rehabilitation and redefinition of the traditional male. Bette Roberts, in her study of Anne Rice, interprets the erotic triangle between Rowan, Michael, and Lasher as a struggle between the head and the heart. Rowan must choose between her emotions, attached to Michael, and her scientific fascination with the newly born Lasher (109). However, the erotic triangle in the novels is perhaps not so simple. The tension between the characters may also be decoded as a contest between two competing views of male behavior and identity, both of which are deconstructed. Michael is representative of the reformed, reclaimed masculinity of gender-conscious, progressive males. However, his identity also maintains much of traditional male behavior. Lasher, paradoxically, occupies the conventional patriarchal role of the male breeder in his sexual exploitation of women. Yet in other ways, he suggests our culture's hysterical fear of feminized men. Critic Ann Larabee has identified Lasher as a completely deconstructed "nature," collapsing the distinction between science and mysticism (175). The same is true of Lasher's gender traits and of those elements in the other principal characters. The novel intentionally problematizes gender-based assumptions about behavior.

Obviously, the contest between the two masculinities is waged over the body of Rowan, who is the empowered contemporary woman, unhindered by obligatory gender codes. She is a professional who is financially and emotionally independent of men; a highly skilled surgeon, she has made her own fortune. Even in her sex life, she maintains her autonomy, choosing partners who are not likely to develop an emotional bond. However, her independence is also physical. She is invulnerable to the violent aggression of males because she has the capacity to kill with her highly developed telepathic abilities. Rowan can cause people to suffer a cerebral hemorrhage merely by becoming angry at them. Among her victims are a fetal-tissue doctor, an attempted rapist, a childhood playmate, and her own father. Rice has clearly attempted to create a woman who is not subject to the physical limitations of traditional femininity. She can and does compete with males at every level.

The clearest manifestation of Rowan's independence from men is apparent in her sexual choices. She desires men who are representative of the most sexist, potentially abusive, and exploitative element of the male population. She specifically desires them for those qualities that are considered most detrimental to the integrity of women's rights:

> I'll take them for their ego and their rambunctiousness, and their ignorance and their rollicking sense of humor; I'll take their roughness and their heated and simple love of women and fear. I'll take their talk.... They don't want you to say anything back to them, they don't even want to know who I am or what I am [*Witching Hour* 110].

Rowan confesses that she likes being treated as a sex object. However, the regressive politics of her longings are mitigated. She too regards her partners as nothing more than eroticized bodies. The key to her contentedness lies in her refusal to accept the subordinate role in gender relations. In Rowan, Rice implies that women's fear of objectification stems from a sense of powerlessness and from a capitulation to social, political, and sexual subjugation. Rowan rises above culturally imposed gender limitations by assuming a position of power, by rejecting the role of eroticized victim, and by manifesting a libidinal appetite that is just as voracious as that of her sexist partners. Rice has even inverted sexual stereotypes by suggesting that some of Rowan's partners were irritated at her treatment of them, such as her refusal to see them again after the first encounter. She is unapologetically promiscuous and indifferent to the emotional subordination of her temporary partners.

Rowan possesses other transgender characteristics, particularly in her professional skills and interests. She intrudes upon the traditionally masculine enterprise of medicine. Yet she outstrips all of her male colleagues with her unparalleled diagnostic and surgical skills. The prioritizing of her profession and her scientific reason over her sexual relationships further undermines gender stereotypes. The sexist tradition of separate spheres for men and women is broken when Rowan chooses to follow Lasher after his birth to study his unusual tissue and DNA. She abandons her domestic commitment to Michael, who almost drowns in the swimming pool.

The thoroughly deconstructed femininity of Rowan calls for an unusual configuration of masculinity in the male to whom she eventually commits herself. Michael's character is constructed upon a series of gender polarities. Rice is making a self-conscious effort to manufacture the progressive masculine specimen who is divorced from traditional sexism, who is not trapped by social conditioning regarding his own gender, but who retains all of the dangerous virility that Rowan regards as sexually desirable. The gender inversion that is inherent in Michael's character is based upon the traditional assumption that the interests and the character traits of cultivated men are more effeminate than those of working-class males (Sinfield *Wilde* 130–56).

In his professional and economic life, Michael is a man of contrasts. By owning a construction company, he is both blue collar and bourgeois. He labors like the working class, but he enjoys the luxuries of immense wealth. He has a few million dollars stashed away, so when his business collapses after his near drowning and subsequent convalescence, he can maintain himself in considerable comfort. He is essentially a self-made wealthy man who still labors to occupy his free time. He does not dabble in the stock market or pursue some other activity that is reminiscent of bored, rich men, but he engages in the most strenuous of activities, construction, which is traditionally associated with the unconscious virility and physical strength of simple men. In Michael, Rowan finds a man who possesses the sheer animal physicality of her usual sexual partners and also matches her own intelligence, wealth, and cultivation. The paradox that lies at the center of Michael's professional interests becomes most evident when the newly engaged couple moves into the decayed house on First Street in New Orleans, part of Rowan's inheritance. Michael is happy to be back at work renovating the old house, but the activity does not appeal exclusively to his desire to remain active. It also fulfills the traditionally feminized need for creative expression. The construction is an aesthetic indulgence (Tsagaris 189). Having always wanted to renovate an old house like the Mayfair home, he finally has the opportunity, and the Mayfair money allows him to pursue the task without any financial limitations (*Witching Hour* 757).

Another dichotomy in his character involves a contrast between the crass and the cultivated: "Michael isn't as stupid as he looks" (204). Michael emerged from Irish-Catholic, working-class stock. All men in his family were firemen, and he feared that he too would have to become a public servant. However, early in his life, Michael discovered high culture. This came first in the form of foreign movies, which he attended with his mother on Saturdays despite the ribbing of his father, who thought that his son was a sissy (41–42). He also developed a love for classical music, which was intensified when he attended a concert by violinist Isaac Stern (48). His interests extended to history and literature. Studying the former in college, he integrated his need for physical labor with his intellectual interests, swinging a hammer and then typing his term papers (57). His love of Charles Dickens, particularly the novel *Great*

Expectations, also found its way into his physical life. He named his construction company after the novel. The polarity between elitist interests and laboring values makes the male protagonist particularly suited for the embraces of Rowan, who is highly educated and yet loves the simplicity and unselfconscious masculinity of blue-collar men. In her former lovers, she had always longed to find a sign of gentility despite her sexual attraction to brutish masculinity. Michael was a "fantasy" to her:

> Rather like imagining that the firefighters she brought home would turn out to be poets, that the policemen she seduced would turn out to be great novelists, that the forest ranger that she'd met in the bar in Bolinas was truly a great painter, and that the husky Vietnam veteran who'd taken her to his cabin in the woods was a great motion picture director hiding from a demanding and worshipful world [138–39].

Despite the effete interests and cultivation of our laboring hero, he is nevertheless a man for whom violence is natural. Michael is a "tough guy with a heart of gold" (65). Rice carefully constructs his character so that he is both sensitive to the feelings of others and prone to physical aggression. Thus, he can be the progressive, gender-conscious male and retain the animal aggression that makes him an exciting sex partner for Rowan. A person for "whom physical action, even of a violent sort, was fairly natural" (39). At the same time, he fears physical aggression:

> In fact, all the violence that he had always sensed simmering around him—in his father, his grandfather, all the men he knew— might rise, like chaos, and drag him down into it [43].

Yet Rice manages to rescue him from effeminacy merely by virtue of his size. He is large enough to play football and make first-string. He holds his own with other men.

Michael's emotional sensitivity is perhaps the most dramatic dismantling of gender stereotypes. This particular attribute is actually quite heavy-handed on the author's part. Michael is prone to excessive grief over lost loves. He cried over his broken relationship with Judith (66), and later he wants to cry in sympathy with Rowan's grief (215). When Rowan departs with Lasher after his birth, Michael becomes severely depressed. Instead of pursuing his wife, he lies around the First Street home, pouting and waiting for her to return. Michael also has maternal instincts. His relationship with Judith ended when she decided to abort a pregnancy against his wishes. Of course, he recognizes her right to do so and "cannot imagine a world in which women do not have such a right" (66), but he is disappointed, wishing that she had carried the child and given it to him when it was born. He would have carried it off where she "would never see either of them again" (67).

Here, Michael's character seems artificial. The author has consciously attempted to create a perfect man who has all of the qualities that are lacking in the traditional male and yet remains the traditional male. He is not a mean between two extremes, involving the compromised diluted features of the polarized masculinities. He is both extremes at the same time. It is neither his sensitivity nor his ruggedness that seems affected, but the suggestion that he could be both at once, that he enjoys violin concertos and brand-new screwdrivers with equal passion seems forced.

It would seem that Rice has salvaged all of the common masculine features to only one end: increased sexual desire. Time and time again, the author likens the sex shared by these two individuals to rape, an interesting analogy since rape has historically been regarded as the ultimate manifestation of gender inequity. Susan Brownmiller describes the crime as "a conscious process of intimidation by which all men keep all women in a state of fear" (quoted in Connell *Gender* 55). So how is it that Rowan could enjoy being raped by her husband? Is this not a manifestation of hegemonic power relations whereby the oppressed actually participates in and condones her own persecution? Why would Rice, whom we have to believe is highly gender conscious, eroticize violence in this way? The first two books of the *Mayfair* series have rape as their central issue. Rowan is a woman who enjoys rough sex and insists upon its similarity to the violent objectification of rape. She desires rugged, working-class men because they serve as the appropriate objects for her violent fantasy. Their uncompromising and selfish masculinity, their voracious sexual appetites, and their powerful bodies compose the profile of an idealized rapist. It is just the physical brawn of Michael, the potential for rape in him, that Rowan desires most: "[I]t was the body that commanded pre-eminence—the bulge in the jeans had to be big enough, the neck powerful, the voice deep, and the coarsely shaven chin rough enough to cut her" (*Witching Hour* 139).

The politics of rape involves power inequities between males and females. Rape necessitates the violent possession of the female by the male, a meeting of power and powerlessness. This paradigm, however, is not appropriate to the rough sex that Rowan and Michael practice. It is true that their encounters are brutal, but they are also consensual. Indeed, Rowan is the principal instigator. Michael enjoys his sex "plain and simple or fancier," depending upon the interests of his partner (65). He does like rough sex when his partner agrees:

> "Ride me hard," she whispered. It was like the slap—a sharp goad that sent his pent-up fury to the boilingpoint. Her fragile form, her tender bruisable flesh—it only incited him. No imagined rape he had ever committed in his secret unaccountable dream soul had ever been more brutal [189].

The above encounter seems to reinforce all of the gender inequality that is a stereotypical feature of rape. Michael is aroused by her vulnerability and his own savageness. Although the author attempts to absolve Michael of any responsibility for his rape fantasies, the passage clearly states that he dreams of forcibly violating women. Rice's situating of this desire within Michael's subconscious seems to invoke the simplistic essentialist argument that all men are natural rapists. But the passage is more complicated than that. Rice suggests that what redeems the encounter and the desire of the participants is not the compromising of Michael's lusty masculinity, but the empowerment of Rowan. She counters Michael's sexual appetite with an equally ferocious desire. The slap that arouses him in the encounter was perpetrated by her, and his desire is intensified by her goading. Rowan suggests that their rough sex involves mutually empowered individuals. She acknowledges that Michael enjoys his sex "rough and tumble the way she did; rather like a rape from both sides" (222). In another passage, she fantasizes about being "tacked to the mattress by an adorable brute" (794). In the second image, the dominance and submission of the sex act is equated to wrestling, a sport in which the participants are paired according to similar size and strength. Of course, Rowan's telekinetic powers constitute a substantial physical equalizer between the two partners; Rowan can kill merely by becoming angry.

The radical feminist stance that all sex is rape because it involves the aggressive possession, penetration, and battering of women by men is not particularly appropriate to Michael and Rowan's relationship. The brutal encounters between the two are more of a testament to Rowan's strength and endurance than to Michael's sexual selfishness and aggressiveness. As a resolution to sexual exploitation, Rice does not offer the symbolic castration of the male. Instead, she presents the empowerment of the female. Her feminism in this context focuses upon the creation of powerful women rather than disempowered men. Thus, she answers one of the most common objections to feminism: that it emasculates the traditional male. With her rape scenes, Rice is able to maintain the traditional masculine stereotype of the lusty male at the same time that she endows him with great sensitivity. She jettisons his arrogance, but she maintains his dangerous virility and sexual appetite. Such a portrayal is a reversal of gender stereotypes wherein males try to wish their sexual fantasies into existence by imagining the woman who is a saint in the kitchen and among the children, but who is a whore in the bedroom. Michael is appropriately tame and docile in the daily interaction of the couple, but he is a madman in bed.

Another form of subordination that antagonizes gender relations and increases the power divide between the sexes is economic. Women's exploitation is grounded in the unequal distribution of wealth between the sexes. Women have historically been dependent upon males as providers, and this form of subjugation contributes to the physical abuse that women endure in our society, an abuse whose most dramatic representation is rape. The economic subordination of women in a capitalist society tends to refuse women's humanity. The socially conditioned male regards the female as an object for his economic and sexual exploitation. Because women are financially dependent, they often do not have the luxury of escaping abusive relationships. In Rice's novel, Rowan is not just financially independent, she is dominant. She controls the huge Mayfair fortune, and it is actually Michael who is somewhat dependent, living in her house and renovating with her money. This further rejection of power inequities confirms Rice's idea that the solution to gender trouble is more powerful women and not necessarily less powerful men.

The interrogation of masculine stereotypes does not end with the portrayal of Michael or with the first novel in the series. *Lasher*, the second novel, is really the story of a serial rapist and murderer. After his birth, the Mayfair ghost, Lasher, is determined to reproduce. Because Rowan is initially incapable of becoming pregnant with his child, he hunts down other Mayfair women who have the family's genetic abnormality. After raping the women, he watches them die as they attempt to give birth to a Taltos. Of course, he is appropriately sorry for their suffering, but he is not sad enough to stop assaulting them because he is bent on reproduction.

Initially, Lasher appears to be the stereotypical womanizing, abusive male. Indeed, he does possess many of those typical personality features. However, his masculinity is a compromised one just like Michael's. In many ways, Lasher represents the thoroughly feminized male, the logical outcome of what some may perceive to be the feminist agenda to reform masculinity. However, Lasher is also the inevitable result of Rowan's peculiar sexual desires. Thus, just like Michael, Lasher seems to combine radically opposing views of manhood. This is not through a synthesis in which each element is compromised. It is through a yoking together of dissimilar, traditionally repelling ideas.

The contrast between Michael and Lasher's masculinities is revealed in the contrast between their appearances. Michael is a powerful, fully developed, middle-aged man who has performed heavy physical labor most of his life. He has the traditional masculine frame, although it is perhaps one reminiscent of a man significantly younger than he is. Nevertheless, he has all of the features of maturity. Lasher, on the other hand, is described as an adolescent with all of the feminine features that the stereotype of the teenage boy includes. He is tall and has long, thin limbs. He is the adolescent boy who has not yet gained the weight proportionate to his height. In addition, Lasher has the long hair that is often the sign of youthful rebellion in men.

One of the most important contrasts between the masculinities of these two men is related to their ages. The men suggest the separation between mature men and boys. The features that Rowan most admires about Michael include his mellowness and his patient attentiveness, both in the bedroom and in their daily lives. The urgency and impatience of Lasher in his selfish, destructive efforts to breed form a sharp contrast to Michael's quiet, supportive assurance. The symbolic youth and infancy of Lasher is most clearly represented by his continual efforts to suckle at his mother's breast (*Lasher* 210). Moreover, the sexual performance of the two men also points out the stereotypical dichotomy in their ages. Michael can only sustain sexual arousal a couple of times a night, while Lasher, like the adolescent male reaching his sexual peak, can perform time and time again. Rowan is not physically capable of accommodating all of Lasher's sexual energy. Michael stoically waits for Rowan's return after she abandons him, while Lasher actively pursues his love objects and then takes violent possession of them without consideration of the consequences for his victims. His efforts to breed seem desperate; his only concern is for himself. In the third novel of the *Mayfair* series, *Taltos*, the ancient Taltos Ashlar classifies Lasher's behavior as the bungling, irrational efforts of a child.

In Lasher, all of Rowan's sexual fantasies are embodied, not in the harmless role-playing of the bedroom, but in his libido. Rowan's desire to be treated as a sex object is more than fulfilled through the violent indifference and abuse of her child. The men whom Rowan desired before meeting Michael were exciting because they seemed dangerous. Their desire for sexual gratification necessitated that they merely use her as a vessel for the enactment of their aggressive fantasies. However, in Lasher, the same type of selfish masculine desire is carried to its logical conclusion. She becomes the prisoner of her and her partner's desire. She loved being "tacked to the mattress" by the lovable brute Michael. With Lasher, she is literally "tacked to the mattress" for four days without food and water while Lasher pursues other wombs to carry his child. In addition, the brawn and potential for violence that she so admired in her former choices is literalized with Lasher. He beats her when she is rebellious. When she attempts to escape, he pummels her into unconsciousness (235). Like the stereotypical abusive spouse, Lasher blames his victim for the physical violence that he uses to subdue her, suggesting that she is culpable for having angered him and that he would not need to beat her if she were more obliging and obedient (206). His selfish exploitation of her body is also reminiscent of her former lovers. He does not care that she has had two miscarriages and that a third might kill her. He is so bent on reproduction that he continues to attempt to impregnate her despite her resistance.

The gendered power inequities that Rice made such an effort to eliminate in the relationship between Michael and Rowan are actually highlighted in the unequal union of Rowan and Lasher. The encounters between Rowan and her husband were merely rough sex that both parties pursued with enthusiasm. Lasher's sexual assaults have all of the classic features of criminal rape. The power divide that was absent from the first relationship is present in the second. Rowan is abducted and forcibly restrained while she is repeatedly and violently raped. The offender has little sympathy for his victim. His only reason for keeping her alive is to guarantee that his child is born through her. The mitigating features that transformed the earlier situation into mutual desire are explicitly eliminated. Rowan's power to kill through telekinesis is ineffective with her captor. Although she was initially drawn to follow Lasher to satiate her scientific interests, she only remains through coercion. She chastises herself for believing that she could patiently endure the abuse of her demon lover in the interests of science. The assaults of Lasher go beyond the physical sex that Rowan and her former lovers enjoyed. This is violence, not desire. Perhaps the most disturbing feature of the sexual exploitation of Rowan is the suggestion that she actually enjoys it despite the threat to her safety. That is, she experiences pleasure during the actual sex act. This comes close to affirming the phallocentric assumption that women enjoy, and perhaps even seek, rape.

The argument that rape is a political crime in which men attempt to assert and sustain their sociopolitical dominance over women is very much applicable to the rape discourse within *Lasher*. Rowan is career oriented, refusing to be confined within the traditional domestic sphere of women. Her restraint and exploitation by Lasher is indicative of the sexist backlash to restore women to their positions of subordination within American society and within the family. Lasher's efforts include forced maternity. Moreover, rather than permitting her to pursue her own interests outside the domestic realm, he literally restrains her so that she will be available only to promote his selfish designs by bearing his children. Lasher becomes a negation of Michael's confident masculinity. Michael waits patiently at home for his wife's return, permits his wife to have a career, and accepts a more domesticated role himself. Lasher's sexual coercion is also social and political. It is the ultimate objectification of women as objects of desire and as objects for economic exploitation. They are unskilled, unpaid labor intended only to facilitate the predominance of men in the social sphere.

The psychoanalytic implications of the love triangle involving Rowan, Michael, and Lasher familiarize the events that, on the surface, seem unusual. As is commonplace within Rice's fiction, the characters are embroiled in the longings and hostilities of the oedipal drama. Lasher's childlike qualities are emphasized in the novel despite the unusual genetic configuration that permits him to mature physically within a matter of moments after his birth. His abduction and repeated rape of his mother, Rowan, literalizes his oedipal longings. From the Freudian perspective, the principal contest within the novel is waged between Michael and Lasher. The child must relinquish his claim on the mother out of fear of castration by the father. However, the traditional power differential between father and son is inverted in this family triangle. Shortly after Lasher's birth, the two men fight for possession of the mother, and the child virtually kills his father. The subsequent episodes that form the plot of the second novel illustrate the consequences of the male child's failure to break the mother-infant dyad and of the child's refusal to obey the social prohibitions against incest that are imposed when the father comes between the mother and the child. The father's interference constitutes the imposition of the law that organizes society, which forces children to choose a mate from a wider gene pool than exists within the immediate family. Lasher's actions reveal a complete disregard for the incest taboo. In addition to the continual rape of his mother, Lasher's other sexual choices are also family members, particularly those who possess the family's genetic abnormality. Lasher may then signify the parent's hysterical fear of producing a sexual renegade, a serial rapist and murderer. On one level, Rice may be attributing his criminal propensities to his inability to navigate successfully the oedipal stage of his psychosexual evolution.

In Freudian theory, the male child who does not successfully break the bond between himself and his mother and begin to identify with his father will become feminized, potentially even becoming a homosexual. The child who does not forsake the mother will not seek mother replacements that are the normative choices for the heterosexual male. This theory formed the basis of the patriarchal account of the origins of homosexuality, an account that sought to blame the female for the son's alternative sexual identity because it was unthinkable that the male could produce a queer child. Historian Martin Duberman, in his autobiography *Cures*, recounts his own run through the psychoanalytic gauntlet, an odyssey that culminated when one of his therapists urged him to break off all communication with his mother without so much as a good-bye. Lasher, after his incarnation, does not seem to be drawn to males as sexual choices. However, while he was still a spirit haunting the Mayfair family, he frequently ravished Julien, one of the few strong males within the family. Although he seems to have no homosexual propensities within the second novel, he is in some ways a thoroughly feminized male. His desperate longing to procreate could be construed as the manifestation of the woman's desire to possess a child within her womb as a replacement for the absent penis. This, however, seems farfetched. It is an example of Freud's pervasive sexism wherein he pathologizes women's sexuality and desire to procreate. Within the context of the novel, Lasher's desire for a child is so desperate that it borders on pathology, suggesting that he feels incomplete without progeny. His own hysterical effort to get a child is set against the quiet excitement and delight that Michael experiences both times that he fathers a child. Although this could once again be an allusion to the age difference between the two men, Lasher's tenacious efforts to impregnate Mayfair women hardly resembles the adolescent male's sexual intensity and aggression, which seldom involves the desire for a child.

Another traditional feminine attribute of Lasher is his emotionality. The assignment of emotion to women and reason to men has formed the basis of gender difference for centuries. Lasher certainly indulges his emotions. He even appears to be unstable in his capricious mood swings that have him crying over Rowan and professing his love for her one moment and then beating her into unconsciousness the next. Another explanation for his behavior may revolve around the emotional instability of children. He is, after all, only a few months old. Such an interpretation may, however, bring us back to where we started because, traditionally, powerful feelings in the male child are coded as feminine and as a weakness to be overcome before he reaches adulthood. Whereas the female child is encouraged to continue her emotional responses to the world, the male is conditioned to suppress his emotions. The only socially accepted outlets for his interior life are anger and desire. Lasher's emotional life also involves the selfishness and cruelty that one associates with children who have not yet learned the norms of social interaction. Certainly self-absorption and violence are traditionally masculine attributes.

Lasher's insatiable sexual appetite is reminiscent of the woman's capacity for multiple orgasms that lies at the heart of men's neurotic fear that they will not be able to satisfy their partners. Men experience anxiety resulting from the knowledge that the measure of manhood is the ability to make women experience sexual satisfaction and climax, but the woman's capacity for multiple orgasms makes these efforts futile. This performance anxiety is heightened by the statistical evidence revealing the proportion of women who have never experienced an orgasm. Lasher's sexual desire seems insatiable, and Rowan fears that the physical consequences of his continued need for sexual stimulation will kill her. The need to procreate drives his sexual desire, a fact that inverts gender stereotypes because it is often the male who has anxiety over his inability to impregnate the female. For a time, Rowan is physically incapable of carrying Lasher's child. When she does finally give birth to Emaleth, the delivery is nearly fatal.

As stated before, the contest between Lasher and Michael for Rowan is symbolically central to the first two novels of the *Mayfair* trilogy. Both men possess deconstructed masculinities that are, nevertheless, at odds with each other. In many ways, Michael's manhood is idealized, a perfect complement to Rowan's masculinized femininity. Lasher, on the other hand, seems to be the logical conclusion of the desire to feminize the male. It takes the male back to infancy before the intrusion of social convention, and it produces a male from the unformed matter of his personality, possessing both uncompromised femininity and masculinity. The result is a creature incapable of functioning within a rule-governed society. Contrary to homophobic propanganda, the complete collapse of gender codes does not result in the modern homosexual. It results in the unprincipled, marauding sex criminal and serial rapist. It is the fear of the fragility of one's own masculinity that leads to aggressiveness toward women and produces the sexual outlaw (Horrocks 89–106).

Sedgewick's theory of male bonding holds that the relationship between the two males in an erotic triangle becomes more important than the relationship between either male and the female. The struggle for dominance over each other is represented in their competition to dominate the woman. Thus, sexual dalliance between either male and the woman becomes symbolic sex between the two males. Rowan's eventual rejection of Lasher and her return to Michael are accompanied by Lasher's destruction, suggesting the repudiation of his abusive masculinity and his unrestrained femininity. Michael sits at the First Street residence, waiting as much for the return of Lasher as for the arrival of Rowan. He is as concerned with exacting his revenge upon the individual who stole his wife as he is with winning her back.

The contest between the two males becomes a combat between rival concepts of masculinity, each revealing a much broader range of experience than the socially constructed notion of manhood usually entails. Michael's quiet, self-assured masculinity, which allows him to display a wide range of traditionally feminine attributes, triumphs over Lasher's wildly erratic, adolescent effort to prove his virility, despite the many potentially feminine traits that motivate his aggression. These two alternative masculinities are obligatory responses to the changing role of women in contemporary society. Of course, Rowan is the embodiment of the new woman who takes on historically male tasks, responsibilities, and skills without apology and without the moment of doubt that socially constituted notions of propriety usually generated. The two male characters offer polarized solutions to the problem of men's conformity in the wake of women's expanded sphere of activities. Michael passively accepts the breakdown of gender categories, modifying his behavior to conform to and complement the new femininity. He has no need or desire to struggle against change. Lasher, on the other hand, rebels against women's social and domestic progress, using violence to force women into domestic and maternal situations. He attempts to restore the old gender hierarchy that viewed women as domestic servants, sex objects, and incubators. Lasher's desperate attempt to hang on to patriarchy reveals a deep-rooted insecurity.

The Lives of the Mayfair Witches seems dedicated to chronicling the collapse of gender distinction and to showing the constructedness of sex roles. From this perspective, the novels, particularly the first two, seem to have a social agenda. The author has made such an officious effort to manufacture both an idealized man and a horrific male that she only succeeds in creating roles as artificial as those that she tries to deconstruct. Even when men are trying to conform to the women's movement or to resist it, rarely are they as passively obliging as Michael or as domineering and openly aggressive as Lasher.

In addition, Rice's use of such broad strokes to salvage Michael's sexual virility in spite of his overtly feminine traits tends to affirm some of the sexism that it tries to dismantle. The sexual aggression that composes Michael's virility is the very passion that has been at the heart of women's protest. Masculine sexual potency and dominance is representative of patriarchal mastery within the social and domestic spheres. The effort to construct Michael as a sexual dynamo despite his passivity in other areas of interaction approaches the hysterical fear that women's progress somehow undermines male virility or that feminism is a threat to men's sexuality. Rowan's sexual appetite confirms the male fantasy that women actually like being raped, that they enjoy the experience when they are raped, and that despite their complaints, women long to be treated as sex objects. To perpetuate such notions is to legitimize the excuse of every date rapist who claimed that his companion really desired him despite her resistance.

The alternative masculinities offered within *The Lives of the Mayfair Witches*, regardless of their sexist implications, seek to expose the femininity lying at the center of traditional manhood and thereby reveal that gender roles are constructed, a reality that once exposed, can then lead to social transformation by expanding the range of activities that are open to both sexes. In a recent study of male gender stereotypes titled *Masculinity in Crisis*, Roger Horrocks describes the fragility of culturally constituted concepts of manhood:

> This is precisely the way I see male identity: It is contradictory, ambivalent. It constantly wrestles with the feminine, absorbs it and then expels it; it purports to be tough, and then reveals its fragility; it seeks to hide neediness and intense feeling—and privately clings to others [48].

Rowan's disappointed rejection of Lasher resonates with meaning when viewed in light of Horrock's observations: "I thought you were something immense, something innocent ... Something wholly unknown and new" (*Lasher* 238). In the new constructions of manhood that Rice offers to her readers, she has only discovered what was always there. The reader examining Rice's ostensibly progressive accounts of the fragility of masculinity finds only a thinly veiled sexism, a capitulation with the very forces that first composed gender division and inequity.

CONCLUSION:
GENDER, HORROR,
AND POPULAR CULTURE

By James R. Keller and Gwendolyn Morgan

Freud observed the recurrent association of the sex and death impulses in the human psyche, which he termed eros and thanatos respectively (Stafford-Clark 192–94). This same combination is manifest in the cross-cultural patterns of transgression and retribution that are found in myth and literature in which those who break society's sexual taboos are subject to violent, frequently grotesque punishments (Osborne ix). The connection also appears in a reverse form, when violent or terrifying events (often unrelated to the sex act itself) have the seemingly incidental result of intense sexual arousal. A third indication of this dynamic is inherent in the politics of rape, a sexual act which is at its heart an expression of aggression, dominance, and rage. Such manifestations have traditionally served to reinforce the patriarchal relationship between the sexes in which the female is submissive and chaste, and the male is dominant and virile.

The most explicit cultural representation of sexual relations is erotic literature and film, particularly pornography. A distinction is drawn here between erotica and pornography. The former is sexually explicit material that also has artistic or intellectual content, while the latter is purely prurient. However, both create debates about sexual politics. Many feminists, like Andrea Dworkin, view pornography as primarily an expression of male exploitation of the female and the perpetuation of the image of woman as merely an object for sexual gratification. Moreover, they contend that pornography encourages sexual aggression against women and is itself a form of violence against women (Dworkin xxxii–xxxiii). Defenders of pornography, on the other hand, suggest that it is necessary for the safe control of sexual tension, providing a release for those energies that may otherwise result in rape and other sexual violence. For some, pornography is considered progressive insofar as it challenges gender stereotyping. It provides visual representations of sexual alternatives, from positions to partners, and it defies the traditional Victorian axiom that women are not supposed to enjoy sex and are supposed to hide their sensual appetites. These opposing voices encounter each other in the struggle over pornography in the age of AIDS. Detractors insist that such explicit material encourages sexual promiscuity, facilitating the proliferation of the disease and compounding the associated social problems. In contrast, defenders maintain that the outlet that pornography and erotica provide for sexual tension reduces indiscriminate promiscuity (McElroy 125–145).

Horror fiction also has its politics. The horrific figure is the outsider who clashes with the representative of normative society. His "crime" against that society is depicted as a violation of law and order. Often, his grotesque physical form symbolizes the transgression of nature and the chaos resulting from its disruption of physical laws. The cultural outsider—whether his trespass is grounded in gender, race, class, religion, politics, or something else—is thus demonized into a monstrous threat to the status quo. Such vilification is intended to turn the public against not only the figure himself, but also the particular ideological or social alternative that he represents. For example, Stoker's Dracula has been seen as a Victorian repudiation of aristocratic decadence, unregulated passion, and female rebellion against culturally imposed limitations.

The established link between eroticism and death has its own politics. According to the normative view, both constitute an obsession that results in the subjugation of all intellectual, social and moral restraint to a particular appetite. In short, they share a loss of control. In the case of pornography, the appetite to be satisfied is lust, and the result is unrestrained eroticism. In the case of horror fiction, the appetite may vary (e.g., megalomania, revenge, money, lust), but it nonetheless results in grotesque violence as the horrific figure attempts to bend society and nature to his whim. The ultimate threat embodied in both is a loss of humanity as those things (i.e., the faculty of reason, the soul, the moral sense) that are construed to separate human from beast, and society from the jungle, succumb to the individual's pursuit of self-gratification. The excess represented in both of these pursuits is particularly insidious to the status quo because it threatens the shared-value systems that organize a society. In consequence, the monster of horror and the participants in pornography are vilified and relegated to the role of social outsider. Admittedly, in horror, the marginalization is primarily an internal mechanic of the fiction (i.e., the monster as demon), while in erotica the guilty parties are those responsible for the industry as a whole: actors, producers, consumers. Nonetheless, each genre partakes of both types of condemnation. Concern about excessive violence and satanic cults moves an increasing number of people to reject the grotesque, particularly in film, and within the fictions of certain pornography, particular groups—primarily women— may be depicted as animalistic, depraved, or merely inferior.

In recent years, much has been said about the impact of "high" art upon the culture that generated it. For instance, new historical analyses of Shakespeare's history plays have shown their impact on shaping subsequent perceptions of the events and characters that they portray. Moreover, society historically tends to assign a value to so-called "high" art that denigrates popular culture, a practice based upon a covert intellectual elitism. Popular culture is not deemed to have sufficient intellectual and artistic subtlety to merit close scrutiny or detailed consideration. This assumes, however, that the perceptions of the so-called cultural elite are those of the majority of society. On the contrary, it seems logical to expect the most influential art to be found in popular culture, which is produced for, and appeals to, a mass audience. Consider that the fiction of Stephen King is more likely to reach a broad audience and to be incorporated into collective responses than the verse of poet laureate Robert Penn Warren is.

The term "popular culture" can be construed in two ways that are not necessarily mutually exclusive: art created for mass consumption or art that is mass-produced. In both cases, the term may refer to popular fiction, music, film, television, and so on. In the past two decades, the belated recognition of mass art's role in the maintenance and subversion of dominant ideologies has led to the establishment of centers, programs, and university courses that are dedicated to the study of popular culture. Today, the relationship between popular culture and sexual politics is particularly important as former watchdogs of gender relations, such as repressive religious and political forces, lose their hold on the populace. Now, mass art often generates and reinforces standards for normative sexual relations, including obligatory heterosexuality, monogamy, family values, and gender constructions, although the latter admittedly has been modified after 30 years of feminist activity.

Anne Rice is a particularly fine example of these dynamics. Her books have been among the best-selling works for almost 25 years, and a number of her books have been converted to film. Indeed, the author and her characters have achieved cult status, and the publication of her novels has become a media event. Moreover, her fiction rides the current wave of interest in vampires and the supernatural, having in large part helped to generate that fascination.

Rice is also truly popular in that she reproduces the polyphonic voice of the culture as a whole, introducing both mainstream ideologies and marginalized discourses in her novels. These alternative voices create a unique tension between progressive and conservative points of view. The resultant ambiguities obscure Rice's own position on the issues and invite the reader to participate in the debate. In *The Vampire Chronicles*, she exploits the traditional association of the vampire with the homosexual to break with impunity the culturally imposed silence on gay issues and thus appears to legitimize marginal subject positions. However, her depictions of the vampire family also perpetuate some of the most damaging homophobic stereotypes, such as pedophilia, promiscuity, predacious sexuality, disease, and sadomasochism. This opposition creates an opportunity for the author to explore both alternative and normative sexuality, including problems with traditional family relations, spouse and child abuse, justifiable homicide, divorce, and gender-power relations.

The Feast of All Saints, Rice's second novel, combines the ubiquitous social issues of race, class, and gender politics by focusing on a community of mixed-race people living in New Orleans before the Civil War. By their very existence, this group dismantles the binary assumptions of American racial ideology. They are politically black while at the same time culturally, sometimes even physically, white. The author illustrates the futile, sometimes even destructive efforts of the community to emulate white culture, concluding that freedom and self-respect can only be achieved by accepting their African heritage. However, this conclusion is oversimplified even in the context of the racial and gender politics of the novel itself. Rice makes a considerable effort to deconstruct the cultural, even physical divide between the ethnic categories within the novel, and then she restores the traditional dichotomy of black and white with the trite identity politics of her conclusion.

In *Cry to Heaven*, Rice seems to advocate unrestrained same-sex eroticism as an acceptable lifestyle choice. However, she also prioritizes heterosexuality, implying that homoerotic activity is the choice of half-men, of ruined heterosexuals. Tonio only shows an interest in other men once he no longer feels physically adequate to pursue women, and the clearest sign of his gradual acceptance of his physical condition is his reawakening ability to consummate his desire for women.

The protagonists of *Exit to Eden* immerse themselves in a world where all of their sadomasochistic fantasies are fully realized. The only erotic dream that cannot be fulfilled at The Club is a monogamous union between two equal partners in love. Lisa and Elliot escape the artifice of The Club's sex games to pursue a conventional relationship. Similarly, Beauty endures a lengthy period of captivity in the Castle, the Village, and the Sultan's Palace, where she is subjected to a battery of dehumanizing erotic games and activities only to be called home to marry and become a traditional wife. Even the structure of the *Beauty* series follows this same pattern. Rice transforms a children's fairy tale into a pornographic, sadomasochistic story of a tortured princess, which is a very subversive project. However, she observes the predominant features of the fairy tale: the conclusion in which the prince and princess live happily ever after, the libidinal nature of the subtext, and the sexist stereotyping of children's literature. Thus, the story is still in large portion a fairy tale with all of the qualities that the genre entails.

Belinda explores the poorly regulated boundary between adolescent and adult sexuality that is constantly breached only to be redrawn. The boundary is perhaps created to encourage a compromise of its own integrity, meaning that adolescence is socially constructed as the vulnerable, eroticized ideal that most adult males desire. Rice offers multiple justifications for reevaluating the age of consent while trying to redefine the boundaries of child abuse by interrogating the assumption that all child loving is exploitative and harmful. A parallel project involves a reevaluating of child pornography laws that designate all nude depictions of children and adolescents as obscene and lacking any redeeming cultural value.

In *The Lives of the Mayfair Witches*, Rice engages the politics of masculine gender construction. Invoking recent interest in the redefinition of masculinity, the author creates two male characters whose attributes subvert traditional masculine behavioral norms. Each is a combination of the progressive and the regressive. Rowan, in her search for a perfect male who combines extreme sexual aggression with social and interpersonal sensitivity, eventually faces a monster, Lasher, who combines physical power and emotional instability. Thus, Rice does not advocate weaker males. She advocates stronger females.

Although Rice raises issues such as racism, myth, economics, and the decline of traditional religions, sexual politics remains the pivotal theme within her work. She addresses virtually all of the most virulent social debates on gender and sexuality. Her decision to adopt such compromising stands on contentious issues may result from any number of forces tugging at her conscience. Her willingness to address subjects that have formerly been anathema within popular culture, particularly at the time that she first began discussing them, in the mid–1970s, may result from a real desire to have a social impact on American culture. There can be no doubt that her work has had a positive impact upon the growing social tolerance for gays and lesbians, despite some of the implications of the fairly heavy-handed parallel between gays and vampirism. One cannot doubt Anne Rice's good will and good intentions toward the gay community. Perhaps Rice's uncompromising acceptance of the gay and lesbian community makes her less self-conscious or guarded in her representations of gay men. Indeed, as her canon of novels has expanded, the portraits of homosexuals have become increasingly ostentatious. The recent *The Vampire Armand* portrays a harem of young boys engaged in libidinous activities.

Much has been said of the author's strict Catholic upbringing and the potential impact of this conditioning on her psyche and her literary imagination. Her consciousness is Catholicism tempered by a humanist disposition. While the recurring imagery of the Catholic mass in her work is frequently employed ironically, the irony is often to the detriment of the unsanctified characters. The religious imagery associated with the vampires is frequently engaged to make them seem more wicked. For example, the association of the vampires' thirst for blood with the Holy Communion serves to accentuate the characters' decadence and their callous disregard for the culture's most sacred institutions. Such a portrayal can have at least two interpretations. The author may desire to portray free spirits who are unfettered by moral restrictions and to expose the hypocrisy of the church, or she may desire to demonstrate the absolute depravity and destructiveness of characters who are unwilling to obey social structures. This latter interpretation is compromised by the appeal of her characters. It is obvious that the reader is supposed to like Lestat despite his decadence and playful wickedness. It is obvious that the author is still mindful of her Catholic upbringing, but the extent to which this influences her conclusion is not at all clear. The tension that this ambiguity creates significantly adds to the richness of her novels.

Rice's interest in contemporary social debates could also be a capitulation to our culture's addiction to novelty. Perhaps she chooses her subjects because she knows that controversy and scandal sells. Witness the market potential of the recent White House sex scandals. One cannot doubt that Rice has discovered a formula for commercial success by combining American's prurient impulses with its love of violence. However, the public may desire novelty and perhaps, at times, even perfidy, but there is likely a limit to its willingness to embrace subversion, particularly sexual subversion. Thus, the author is forced to compromise her conclusions to retain the profitability of her work. Even the strongest stomachs have difficulty with some of the situations in the *Beauty* series, but the conventional conclusions of the trilogy tend to abate the sexually seditious subject matter. Rice's project to demonstrate that sex is not dirty, that it is even potentially therapeutic, is advanced by her negotiated conclusion. By showing that those who have engaged in even the most dehumanizing debauchery can still achieve a happy marital union, the author deflates the cultural presumption that sex is damaging, especially to the young.

Finally, the negotiation between popular and elitist culture in Rice's novels is the one that makes this book possible. The author adopts two of the literary genres that are most frequently associated with low culture, horror and erotica, and lends an intellectual integrity to them that is characteristic of high cultural practices. Her vampires, witches, and sexual renegades are also philosophers, historians, and poets. This combination enables her to be taken seriously while becoming an extraordinary commercial success, transforming the literati into advocates of popular fiction and the casual readers into literary critics.

BIBLIOGRAPHY

Abelove, Henry. "Freud, Male Homosexuality, and the Americans." In *The Lesbian and Gay Studies Reader*. Eds. Henry Abelove, Michele Aina Barale, David M. Halpern. New York: Routledge, 1993. 381–93.

Auerbach, Nina. *Our Vampires Ourselves*. Chicago: University of Chicago Press, 1995.

Babb, Valerie. *Whiteness Visible: The Meaning of Whiteness in American Literature and Culture*. New York: New York University Press, 1998.

Bakhtin, Mikhail. *Rabelais and His World*. Trans. Helene Iswolsky. Bloomington: Indiana University Press, 1984.

Bayer, Ronald. *Homosexuality and American Psychiatry: The Politics of Diagnosis*. Princeton: Princeton University Press, 1987.

Califia, Pat. *Public Sex*. Pittsburgh: Cleis, 1994.

Chancer, Lynn S. *Sadomasochism in Everyday Life*. New Brunswick, NJ: Rutgers University Press, 1992.

Connell, R. W. *Gender & Power*. Stanford: Stanford University Press, 1987.

_____. *Masculinities*. Berkeley: University of California Press, 1995.

Dollimore, Jonathan. *Sexual Dissidence*. Oxford: Clarendon, 1991.

Duberman, Martin. *Cures: A Gay Man's Odyssey*. New York: Dutton, 1991.

Dworkin, Andrea. *Pornography: Men Possessing Women*. New York: Plume, 1979.

Dyer, Richard. "Children of the Night: Vampirism as Homosexuality, Homosexuality as Vampirism." *Sweet Dreams: Sexuality, Gender, and Popular Fiction*. Ed. Susannah Radstone. London: Lawrence & Wisehart, 1988. 47–72.

Edwards, Tim. *Erotics and Politics: Gay Male Sexuality, Masculinity, and Feminism*. Ed. Jeff Hearn. New York: Routledge, 1994.

Felman, Shoshana. "On Reading Poetry: Reflections on the Limits and

167

Possibilities of Psychoanalytic Approaches." *The Purloined Poe: Lacan, Derrida, and Psychoanalytic Reading*. Ed. John P. Muller and William J. Richardson. Baltimore: Johns Hopkins University Press, 1988. 133–156.

Foucault, Michel. *The Care of the Self*. Trans. Robert Hurley. New York: Vintage, 1986.

_____. *Discipline and Punish: The Birth of the Prison*. Trans. Alan Sheridan. New York: Vintage, 1979.

_____. *The History of Sexuality: An Introduction*. Vol. 1. Trans. Robert Hurley. New York: Vintage, 1978.

Freud, Sigmund. *The Ego and the Id*. Ed. James Strachey. Trans. Joan Riviere. New York: Norton, 1960.

_____. *Three Essays on the Theory of Sexuality*. Standard Edition. Vol. 7. London: Hogarth, 1953. 125–245.

Gallop, Jane. *Reading Lacan*. Ithaca: Cornell University Press, 1985.

Gelder, Ken. *Reading the Vampire*. New York: Routledge, 1994.

Greenberg, David F. *The Construction of Homosexuality*. Chicago: University of Chicago Press, 1988.

Greenblatt, Stephen J. *Learning to Curse: Essays in Early Modern Culture*. New York: Routledge, 1990.

Haas, Lynda, and Robert Haas. "Living With(out) Boundaries: The Novels of Anne Rice." *A Dark Night's Dreaming: Contemporary American Horror Fiction*. Eds. Tony Magistrale and Michael A. Morrison. Columbia: University of South Carolina Press, 1996. 55–67.

Halperin, David M. "Sex Before Sexuality: Pederasty, Politics and Power in Classical Athens." *Hidden from History: Reclaiming the Gay and Lesbian Past*. Eds. Martin Duberman, Martha Vicinus, and George Chauncy. New York: Meridian, 1989. 37–53.

Hanson, Ellis. "Undead." *Inside/Outside: Lesbian Theories, Gay Theories*. Ed. Dianna Fuss. New York: Routledge, 1991.

Hennegan, Alison. "On Becoming a Lesbian Reader." *Sweet Dreams: Sexuality, Gender, and Popular Fiction*. Ed. Susannah Radstone. London: Larence & Wishart, 1988. 165–190.

Hodges, Devon, and Janice L. Doane. "Undoing Feminism in Anne Rice's *Vampire Chronicles*." In *Modernity and Mass Culture*. Ed. James Naremore and Patrick Brantlinger. Bloomington: Indiana University Press, 1990. 159–75.

Hoppenstand, Gary, and Ray B. Browne, eds. *The Gothic World of Anne Rice*. Bowling Green, OH: Bowling Green University Press, 1996.

Horrocks, Roger. *Masculinity in Crisis: Myths, Fantasies and Realities*. New York: St. Martin's Press, 1994.

Irigaray, Luce. *This Sex Which Is Not One.* Trans. Catherine Porter. Ithaca: Cornell University Press, 1985.

Jordan, Neil, dir. *Interview with the Vampire.* Warner Bros., 1994.

Kincaid, James R. *Child-Loving: The Erotic Child and Victorian Culture.* New York: Routledge, 1992.

Kinlaw, Marty, and Cynthia Kasee. "Degrees of Darkness: *Gens de Couleur Libre* Ethnic Identity in *The Feast of All Saints.*" In *The Gothic World of Anne Rice.* Eds. Gary Hoppenstand and Ray B. Browne. Bowling Green, OH: Bowling Green University Press, 1996. 215–30.

Lacan, Jacques. *Ecrits.* Trans. Alan Sheridan. New York: Norton, 1977.

_____. "Seminar on *The Purloined Letter.*" Trans. Jeffrey Mehlman. *French Freud: Structural Studies in Psychoanalysis,* Yale French Studies 48, 1972. 38–72.

Larabee, Ann. "'We're Talking Science, Man, Not Voodoo': Genetic Disaster in Anne Rice's *Mayfair Witch Chronicles.*" In *The Gothic World of Anne Rice.* Eds. Gary Hoppenstand and Ray B. Browne. Bowling Green, OH: Bowling Green University Press, 1996. 173–83.

Lee, Jonathan Scott. *Jacques Lacan.* Amherst: University of Massachusetts Press, 1990.

LeFanu, J. Sheridan. "Carmilla." *The Penguin Book of Vampire Stories.* Ed. Alan Ryan. Harmondsworth: Pengin, 1988.

Levi-Straus, Claude. *The Elementary Structure of Kinship.* Ed. Rodney Needham. Trans. James Harle Bell and John Richard von Sturmer. Boston: Beacon, 1969.

Liberman, Terri R. "Eroticism as the Moral Fulcrum in Rice's *Vampire Chronicles.*" *The Gothic World of Anne Rice.* Eds. Gary Hoppenstand and Ray B. Browne. Bowling Green, OH: Bowling Green University Press, 1996. 109–21.

Marshall, Garry, dir. *Exit to Eden.* HBO, 1994.

McElroy, Wendy. *XXX: A Woman's Right to Pornography.* New York: St. Martin's, 1995.

Miller, Robin. "The Real World of the Free People of Color in Anne Rice's *The Feast of All Saints.*" In *The Anne Rice Reader: Writers Explore the Universe of Anne Rice.* Ed. Katherine Ramsland. New York: Ballantine, 1997. 212–24.

Morris, David B. *The Culture of Pain.* Berkley: University of California Press, 1991.

Muller, John P., and William J. Richardson, eds. *The Purloined Poe: Lacan, Derrida, and Psychoanalytic Reading.* Baltimore: Johns Hopkins University Press, 1988.

Osborne, Lawrence. *The Poisoned Embrace: A Brief History of Sexual Pessimism.* New York: Pantheon, 1993.

O'Toole, Laurence. *Pornocopia: Porn, Sex, Technology, and Desire.* New York: Serpent's Tail, 1998.

Ragland-Sullivan, Ellie. *Jacques Lacan and the Philosophy of Psychoanalysis.* Urbana: University of Illinois Press, 1986.

Ramsland, Katherine. "Forced Consent and Voluptuous Captivity: The Paradoxical Psychology Behind Anne Rice's Erotic Imagination." In *The Anne Rice Reader: Writers Explore the Universe of Anne Rice.* Ed. Katherine Ramsland. New York: Ballantine, 1997: 322–46.

_____. *Prism of the Night: A Biography of Anne Rice.* New York: Plume, 1992.

Rice, Anne. *Beauty's Punishment.* New York: Plume, 1984.

_____. *Beauty's Release.* New York: Plume, 1985.

_____. *Belinda.* New York: Jove, 1986.

_____. *The Claiming of Sleeping Beauty.* New York: Plume, 1983.

_____. *Cry to Heaven.* New York: Ballantine, 1982.

_____. *Exit to Eden.* New York: Dell, 1985.

_____. *The Feast of All Saints.* New York: Ballantine, 1979

_____. *Interview with the Vampire.* New York: Ballantine, 1976.

_____. *Lasher.* New York: Ballantine, 1993.

_____. *Memnoch the Devil.* New York: Knopf, 1995.

_____. *The Queen of the Damned.* New York: Ballantine, 1988.

_____. *The Tale of the Body Thief.* New York: Knopf, 1992.

_____. *The Vampire Armand.* New York: Knopf, 1998.

_____. *The Vampire Lestat.* New York: Ballantine, 1985.

_____. *The Witching Hour.* New York: Ballantine, 1990.

Riley, Michael. *Conversations with Anne Rice: An Intimate Enlightening Portrait of Her Life and Her Work.* New York: Ballantine, 1996.

Roberts, Bette. *Anne Rice.* New York: Twayne, 1994.

_____. "The Historical Novels of Anne Rice." In *The Gothic World of Anne Rice.* Eds. Gary Hoppenstand and Ray B. Browne. Bowling Green, OH: Bowling Green University Press, 1996. 197–213.

Rout, Kay Kinsella. "The Least of These: Exploitation in Anne Rice's *Mayfair Witch* Trilogy." *Journal of American Culture* 19 (1996): 87–93.

Sarup, Madam. *Jacques Lacan.* Toronto: University of Toronto Press, 1992.

Sedgewick, Eve Kosofsky. *Between Men: English Literature and Male Homosocial Desire.* New York: Columbia University Press, 1985.

Segal, Lynne. *Slow Motion: Changing Masculinities, Changing Men.* New Brunswick, NJ: Rutgers University Press, 1990.

Silverman, Kaja. "The Lacanian Phallus." *Differences* 4 (Spring 1992): 84–115.

Sinfield, Alan. *Faultlines: Cultural Materialism and the Politics of Dissident Reading.* Berkeley: University of California Press, 1992.

_____. *The Wilde Century: Effeminacy, Oscar Wilde, and the Queer Moment.* New York: Columbia University Press, 1994.

Stafford-Clark, David. *What Freud Really Said.* New York: Schocken, 1965.

Stallybrass, Peter, and Allon White. *The Politics and Poetics of Transgression.* Ithaca: Cornell University Press, 1986.

Treichler, Paula A. "AIDS, Homophobia, and Biomedical Discourse: An Epidemic of Significations." *AIDS: Cultural Analysis, Cultural Activism.* Ed. Douglas Crimp. Cambridge: Massachusetts Institute of Technology University Press, 1987. 31–70.

Tsagaris, Ellen M. "'He's Not One of Them': Michael Curry and the Interpellation of the Self in Anne Rice's *The Witching Hour.*" In *The Gothic World of Anne Rice.* Eds. Gary Hoppenstand and Ray B. Browne. Bowling Green, OH: Bowling Green University Press, 1996. 185–95.

Tsang, D., ed. *The Age of Taboo: Gay Male Sexuality—Power and Consent.* London: Gay Men's Press, 1981.

Van Herik, Judith. *Freud on Femininity and Faith.* Berkeley: University of California Press, 1982.

Ziv, Amalia. "The Pervert's Progress: An Analysis of the *Story of O* and the *Beauty* Trilogy." *Feminist Review* 46 (1994): 61–75.

INDEX